Navigating The
First Six
Weeks

— • • • • • —

What new parents need to know!

DR. KATE STEELE, FANZCA, MBBS (QLD), BSc
NICK MANNING, BBUS(COMN)

CONTENTS

ABOUT THE AUTHORS

Dr. Kate Steele is a consultant anaesthetist who has practiced in both the United States of America and Australia. Her fellowship was undertaken in obstetric anaesthesia. It remains an active interest. Nick Manning is the author of over 40 published books.

Nick and Kate also happen to be married and have a baby. It's the reason they started researching this book—that's their little girl on the front cover!

ABOUT THIS BOOK

This book is REAL

It's designed to give new parents effective and realistic advice that will help them cope with a time in their lives that is both wonderful and brutal in equal measures.

It doesn't pull any punches. It talks about the good stuff and the bad stuff, because the authors firmly believe that being a parent is *hard*... but being prepared helps. This book contains confronting information about what it's really like to be a parent! But rest assured—the journey will get easier.

This book *doesn't* have all the answers

Knowing that most new parents are time poor, this book was designed to orient you to the world of babies as fast as possible. Some chapters are short. You don't need padding! You need enough information to be prepared and informed, but not so much that you feel like you're reading a technical report.

In this book, we'll tell you what we feel you *need* to know, then provide links to further reading, should you wish to delve deeper.

This book is evidence based

All facts, figures and advice in this book are based on research, unless stated otherwise (occasionally, we'll give our opinions as fellow parents, but when we do we'll try to say something like 'in our experience, this is what happened').

Source material for each chapter is listed in an appendix at the end of the book.

This book says what nobody else tells you

"Don't drop your baby. Make sure you bathe them. Regularly change their nappies."

All of this is important, but it's also advice that anyone can tell you. You'll find this information in a million baby books out there on the market.

So... you won't find it here. Including everything there is to know about newborns would make this book the size of an encyclopedia (and you'd fall asleep while reading it).

Instead, within these pages, we focus on the things that take many people by surprise when they have a newborn. Things like the concept of the fourth trimester, cluster feeding, and what the REAL difference is between breastfeeding and formula.

Think of this book as a quick and succinct guide to 'what's not in the brochure.'

LEGAL DISCLAIMER

No two babies on this planet are the same. Even identical twins have differences in personality! Therefore, the information in this book is given as general advice only and you should consult a qualified health professional to determine what is appropriate for you and your baby.

This book has been checked by a pediatrician, nurse, midwife, psychologist and anesthetist. A lot of effort has been put into its accuracy and advice, but that doesn't mean we know your circumstances or can advise specifically on them.

The contents of this book, including medical opinions and any other health-related information, is for informational purposes only and should not be considered a specific diagnosis or treatment plan for any individual situation. Use of this book and the information contained herein does not create a doctor-patient relationship.

Occasionally, this book will say words like 'your baby' when describing the actions of an infant. Obviously, the authors don't know your baby personally, so please take this as a description of babies in general, with no guarantee that your child will match this description exactly.

Finally (and thank you for reading this far) throughout this book you will find quotes from other parents. Any information given within these quotes should not be construed as advice, but rather simply as a description or opinion of how this grand, glorious, wonderful journey that is parenthood worked for that very specific family.

INTRODUCTION

The human mind is a wonderful thing. Already, as we write this introduction, those first six weeks after the birth of our own little girl seem like a distant memory. We can barely remember the terror and confusion that went hand in hand with the overwhelming joy that marked the birth of our baby daughter.

There's just so much to do and know when you have a baby! Suddenly so many things that seemed unimportant just nine months prior become critical in the weeks leading up to the birth:

Should I breastfeed?
What do I need to buy?
What's the deal with formula?
And what the heck is SIDS?

After your child is born, life becomes a whirlwind. And funnily enough, more questions pop up—things you hadn't considered even weeks ago, but that now feel impossibly urgent:

How do I stop my child crying?
How do I get my child to sleep better?
She's losing weight—is that bad?
And when will she smile?

Here's the brutal truth—for the unprepared, the first six weeks are *hard*. Your child has to learn to live in this world, and that responsibility to guide his or her transition will weigh heavily on your shoulders.

You'll survive whether you read this book or not—billions of other people on this planet have. But... it's our hope that this book will make that journey easier, with answers to questions you may not even know to ask.

Within this book's pages you'll find heavily researched, evidence-based advice on what you really need to know when having a child. There are a couple of opinions scattered here and there—we try to acknowledge them as such when we make them—but for the most part the information contained herein is based on professional recommendations and backed by research.

Our deepest thanks go out to the pediatricians, midwives, doctors, psychologists and other health care professionals that have helped shape and proof-read this book. With their assistance, we hope we've given you the tools to make those first six weeks just that little bit smoother.

- Dr. Kate Steele, *FANZCA, MBBS (QLD), BSc*
- Nick Manning, *BBus(Comn) (Distinction)*

1 | THE FIRST 6 WEEKS

We couldn't believe it when they let us walk out of the hospital with our newborn. We kept looking at each other in disbelief, as if to say, 'don't they know we have no idea what we're doing?'

New parents get all this pre-birth advice, these classes and lessons. But then the baby comes and suddenly you're walking out of the hospital with this tiny little bundle, and it feels like there should have been an exam before that happened.

We kept waiting for someone to stop us and go 'hey, what do you think you're doing, you can't take that out of here! You're not qualified to do this!'

JIM, FATHER OF ETHAN

Let's start this book with the ice-cold bucket of water that is the first six weeks. Really, the contents of this entire book cover this month and a half timeframe, but it's such an important concept to understand that we've made it a chapter all on its own.

The first six weeks will be the most wonderful, terrifying, heart melting, brain frying time of your life. And unless you already have children, the way it all unfolds will be one heck of a surprise.

For first-time parents, the first six weeks are hard. They are often unprepared, not only by how different their lives have suddenly become, but also by how unlike 'a baby' their little one is. That sounds strange, we know. He or she *is* a baby, right?

Before we answer that, let's try an experiment.

Close your eyes briefly and imagine your newborn. What will they look like? What will they say? Can you imagine them burbling happily while you change their diaper? Perhaps the image that appears is of you gazing deeply in their eyes as they smile? Maybe you envision the little one reaching out to grip your finger. All these things sound amazing, right? Bet you can't look forward to experiencing them.

And they *are* amazing. The first time your child smiles at you just makes the entire day better. And hearing your baby laugh? There's nothing quite like it.

The thing is though, your baby won't smile until around six to eight weeks. They'll only start cooing around the same time,[1] and they won't laugh until around four months.[2] When your baby is first born, they don't know that their hands are part of their body. They can only lift their head very briefly,[3] so won't be sitting up and playing patty-cake with you anytime soon!

For the first six weeks, a baby isn't really a baby as we think of one. They're still growing into that—human babies take months after birth to learn many of the things that other animals are born with![4] The chapter titled *The Fourth Trimester* covers this concept in more detail, but for now what you need to know is this: all those interactions that most first time parents associate with babies happen *after* the first six weeks. Beforehand? Babies are literally all work and no play, and much of the feedback they'll give a new parent seems negative—because they'll cry when something's wrong but can't yet smile when they're happy. Sometimes, it seems their only talents are breathing, eating, crying and pooing.

Lucky they're cute.

2 | MILESTONES ARE VARIABLE

It's easy to be lulled by milestones. The comfort they bring is from a sense of control—that you have an itinerary for what your child will be doing.

The problem, of course, is that babies don't have calendars. They don't know they need to discover their fingers at six weeks or start crawling at six months! I keep telling my baby girl she needs to set reminders, but so far she's refused to listen.

JANICE, MOTHER OF SCARLETT

Before we get into this book properly, it's important to remember that any developmental milestone you ever read about in this book or any other is just an approximation. Your child may master that skill earlier or later, and that's usually perfectly fine and normal. This doesn't just apply in the first six weeks but for the coming months and years as well.

Many parents experience unnecessary stress when their child's development doesn't marry exactly with guidelines. The value of milestones lies in preparing a parent for what to expect, not what to demand of the child, and for alerting caregivers to seek a professional opinion if their child falls too far outside what's considered to be normal.

So, when should you start to worry? It turns out that in addition to milestones, which are designed to give you a *general* indicator, pediatricians also have *specific* referral guidelines for when to come and see them. Different countries have different variations on these guidelines: our favorite is the Australian 'red flag' guidelines because of how easy they are to understand. The American CDC has also developed an app which you may find useful.

Parents should be able to find these guidelines for other countries by typing the name of their country into Google along with the words 'red flag developmental guidelines,' but it should be noted that if you *ever* have strong concerns about the development of your child (at any age), it's wise to talk to a health professional.

3 | THE FOURTH TRIMESTER

I didn't really understand the Fourth Trimester theory before my child was born. But as I held her and I realized just how fragile and helpless she was, it all made perfect sense. There's something delicate about our babies. Other newborn animals may look cute, but humans look truly helpless.

I've never been as gentle, doting or over-protective with anything as I was with my own daughter. And this instinct kicked in before I realized what I was doing. Thank goodness.

TERRY, FATHER OF ISLA

The fourth trimester is a relatively new concept that's quickly gaining momentum. In a nutshell, the theory suggests that human babies, from a growth perspective, are really born about three months too early.[5]

This might sound strange—who ever heard of a one-year pregnancy?—but there's a lot of truth to the theory. In most other mammals, newborns are much more capable than our species. Baby cows can walk, giraffes fall up to six feet to the ground and survive, and almost every other mammal can move from where they're born to their food source as soon as they leave the womb.

Human babies can't do that. The leading theory as to *why* is that we're too smart. Our brains are so large (comparative to our bodies) that delaying a birth any later than nine months would mean that our mothers couldn't birth us.[a] So, the mother's body evicts the baby before it's truly ready.

Once free of the mother, a baby develops at an astonishing rate. The three months after birth, where an infant learns many of the skills that will eventually assist in his ability to care for himself—to grasp with his hands, track moving objects and make rudimentary sounds to name a few—is called the fourth trimester.

---

[a] *It pays to note that there are conflicting theories on the reason a child leaves the womb early: some scientists believe it's not brain size but the mother's ability to supply their child with enough energy to keep growing that could cause an evolutionary 'early' birth. For more information on this theory, see: https://six-weeks.com/links#3*

WHY THIS IS IMPORTANT

Understanding the concept of the fourth trimester teaches parents what to expect from and how to fulfill the needs of newborn babies. When a newborn baby has just learned to breathe, don't expect her to sit up, focus on your face or smile!

During the first six weeks your baby is 100% helpless. Not only will you be feeding her and changing nappies, but you'll also have to monitor her temperature, hold her head stable when you move her, comfort her, and rock her to sleep. Moreover, your baby has just come from a safe, warm, comforting environment where she was fed 24 hours a day. But now, everything feels different, there's too much space around her body, and for the first time ever, she's hungry.

What does this mean? First, you're going to be busy! Your every waking moment will be spent caring for your baby. *Like, every moment.* Except (maybe) when you're asleep.

Second, you've just been given a secret cheat that lets you easily comfort her! Rocking your child, swaddling her in a wrap and playing 'white noise' all mimic conditions that remind the baby of the womb. She's been out for so little time that experiencing these things will still soothe her. See the *How to calm a crying baby* chapter for more information.

FURTHER INFORMATION:

The Fourth Trimester (Book)
A highly detailed look into the theory behind the fourth trimester, including evidence-based research to support the theory, and descriptions of what an infant experiences (and how he or she develops) over the first 12 weeks.

The Happiest Baby on the Block (Book)
Although focused mainly around soothing babies and increasing their sleep, Dr. Karp is a strong believer in the fourth trimester and discusses it in early chapters, using it as a platform from which to develop his techniques.

Please see https://six-weeks.com/links#3 for web links.

4 | BABY WEIGHT

The first thing people ask when you have a baby is "what does she weigh?" It's also the first thing people comment on when they see her: "oh, that's a big baby," or "oh, what a tiny little girl."

Nobody goes "hey, how many inches is she?" I think it's because there are so few standards by which to measure a child's health. It's like our caveman brain kicks in and goes 'Thin baby bad. Fat baby good.'

BRUCE, FATHER OF JOEY

Babies lose weight before they put gain weight. And no, not just because of the massive black poo your child will do after he or she is born (seriously, the poo looks like tar—search for 'meconium' online, or check out a baby poop guide[b]).

Most babies who are born full-term (38-40 weeks gestation) weigh between 6-9 lbs (2.72-4.08kg) though they can be born outside this and still be completely healthy! After being born, it's expected that they'll lose a little weight in the first 5-7 days of life.[6] This can cause stress for some parents—especially as hospitals monitor this quite closely—but don't worry, it's completely normal.

For the last nine months, your child has had perfect nutrition 24 hours a day, courtesy of the mother and her placenta. But after birth, your baby will start to lose weight until nourishment from the milk kicks in.

As a rule of thumb, a 5% weight loss is considered normal for a formula-fed newborn and a 7-10% loss is considered normal for breastfed babies,[7] though some hospitals have more specific guidelines. The difference in weight loss between breastfed and formula fed babies is due to breastmilk often taking a few days to come in, versus formula is instant. Weight loss is also dependent on factors that can be specific to each baby—for example, prematurity, or specific health issues.

---

[b] *We've linked one at https://six-weeks.com/links#4*

Pediatricians, midwives, child health clinics and medical staff all keep a sharp eye on newborn weight as drops above normal can be a signifier of insufficient milk supply and general health issues. The best method of measuring an infant's weight is with baby scales—most general practices, pharmacies and child health clinics allow you to measure your infant's weight using these. A less-precise alternative is to use adult scales: weigh yourself carrying the baby, then yourself alone, and subtract one figure from the other to get your baby's weight. If you have any concerns when measuring your child's weight using adult scales, be sure to double check their weight with infant scales. You can then go to online resources such as the *Newborn Weight Tool* (see the further information section at the end of this chapter) to monitor their progress.

Use tools like this with your 'sensible hat' firmly on—weight can vary greatly between babies and just because your child doesn't sit exactly on the average line, or average *centile* (which is another way of saying *percentile*, meaning *how your child compares to other children her age*) doesn't mean they aren't perfectly healthy. What doctors are really looking for here are extreme outliers and fluctuations—babies that begin dropping weight dramatically when other babies aren't, for example.

The easiest way to think about this is to remember back to class photos when you were at school. The tallest person would be put at one end of the line and the shortest at the other, and it didn't really matter where you stood because you'd still be in the photo. Usually though, you could expect to be standing next to the same person the following year.

Centiles are a little like this in that your baby's height, weight and other variables are put on a graph and measured against other infants, and *it doesn't matter where your baby is on the line*, only that they keep that 'position' as they grow. Medical professionals become concerned if a child grows really quickly and shoots past everyone else, or if they don't grow as fast and everyone else grows past them.

Our own child measured on the 23rd centile for weight after birth (that is, in the bottom 23% of all children, meaning she was very small) and while she did gain weight rapidly, the change wasn't fast enough vs. the weight other babies were putting on to cause doctors any concern.

Her head circumference was a different matter. Starting with a very small head (she was on the 2nd centile, meaning she was in the lowest 2% of head size compared to other children her age), she rocketed up to the 80th centile over a seven-month period. Both the 2nd centile and the 80th centile would have been fine if she charted consistently along this line, but her rapid change between them triggered a need to scan her head to ensure it wasn't growing rapidly for the wrong reasons (like a tumor). We're pleased to say that everything was fine—she just has a big head. It runs in the family!

Be careful to use the same set of scales when measuring your infant's weight each time—household scales are rarely calibrated exactly, and you don't want the difference between two sets of scales to affect your measurements.

If you don't have access to scales, keep an eye on wet diapers. A baby in their first six weeks should be wetting their diaper regularly, because this means they're taking in enough milk to keep themselves hydrated, and this is one of the most important reasons newborn weight is monitored.

A newborn should wet their diaper at least once on day 1, twice on day 2, three times on day 3, etc. —all the way up to six times a day, by day 6. After that, you should expect your newborn to wet their diaper at least six times a day from then on (or five times if they're wearing disposables).[8]

As with all things baby related, if you're worried about your baby's weight loss, look for a child health clinic or talk to a doctor—it's always better to be safe than sorry.

Tip: Well-Baby Clinics

Many countries have something called a 'well-baby' checkup, where new parents are encouraged to get their baby assessed for healthy development at regular intervals (for example at four weeks, eight weeks and then four months of age). The checks may be done by health workers, midwives, GPs, or pediatricians depending on your country.

It's well worth investigating if there are clinics near where you live, as they will allow you to monitor, among other things, your baby's weight.

FURTHER INFORMATION:

Newt: Newborn Weight Tool (Website)
This website allows parents to see how a newborn's weight during the first days and weeks following childbirth compares with a large sample of other newborns. As stated previously, use websites like this with your sensible hat firmly on—it's a great tool, but doesn't take account

of a child's sex, whether it was born prematurely, health issues or ethnicity (all of which can influence weight).

Feed & Diaper/Nappy Chart (PDF)

A printout that lets you chart your newborn's feeds, wet diapers and bowel movements in the first 16 days. Lists like these are unnecessary for healthy babies. However if you're worried about your child's progress, something like this can be very useful.

Please see https://six-weeks.com/links#4 for web links.

5 | SLEEPLESS NIGHTS

Parenting is a team sport in all areas but one. We take turns changing nappies and bathing our son, but when the lights go out it's every man or woman for themselves.

On TV shows, if the baby is crying one parent will roll to the other and say, "it's your turn to get up." But when you're getting less sleep in a week than you previously did in a night, teamwork quickly degenerates into a game of 'who can pretend to sleep the longest.'

Don't get me wrong—I love my wife and child. But that doesn't stop me lying with my eyes closed, praying my wife stirs before I do. She's doing the same, of course!

Eventually one person sighs and gets up, making it clear they know the other is awake. Because to the victor goes the chance to sleep for four hours, not three. Before we had our son that was a trifle. But now? People who say they sleep like a baby obviously don't have one.

JOSÉ, FATHER OF NICOLÁS

Everyone's heard that new parents don't get much sleep, but here's the kicker—whatever you're thinking, or whatever you assume, it's almost guaranteed to be *worse than you think.*

The problem with what people know about sleep deprivation in the first six weeks is that much of the data, given by friends and relatives, is tinted by rose-colored glasses. Oxytocin, one of the hormones released after pregnancy and during breastfeeding, has an amnestic effect on human memory.[9] Fathers can also experience surges in oxytocin just from assisting with childcare.[10] This may be one of the reasons that memory loss is experienced not just by mothers, but also by fathers. Put another way: our bodies are very good at getting us to forget the bad times after birth. Think of it as a genetic trait for human survival.

So, what's the real deal? You may have read that new babies sleep up to 16 hours a day. That means you'll get plenty of sleep, right? And even if you don't, what's so hard about a couple of sleepless nights?

Let's start by giving an example from the authors' personal experience. Coming into the birth of our child, we were well prepared to handle sleep deprivation. Between us we've experienced glandular fever, also known as mono (a disease that teaches you what it's like to be extremely tired), medically diagnosed insomnia (a condition that teaches you to survive on very little sleep), military training (a profession that makes a point of teaching you to survive on minimal sleep), medical training (a profession that helps you understand the effects of minimal sleep through experience) and we've both had jobs that regularly required us to work through the night, sometimes for up to 40 hours straight.

Then the birth of our child came along.

And we were absolutely shattered.

We've never been so tired—couldn't even imagine being so tired—than we were in those first six weeks. Life was a fugue of sleepless nights, dirty nappies and feeding that just went on and on and on. Without respite.

Newborns sleep *a lot*. But their sleep is in very short segments,[11] in some cases waking every 20 minutes! This means that while the baby might get 16 hours sleep in total, parents most certainly will not. Worse, if you have a newborn that sleeps for more than 4-5 hours in the first few weeks you may need to wake your little sleeper up to help them feed and put on weight!

There are many reasons why infants sleep in short bursts, but one practical one has to do with the capacity of your baby's stomach. The size of a marble at birth, it's no wonder infants wake so often to feed—they can barely fit anything in! Their stomach grows quickly in those first 10 days, but until it does, those sleepless nights are hard. To illustrate the point, here's our daughter's sleep and feed schedule on days 3, 10 and 17—i.e., halfway through weeks 1, 2 & 3. If reading columns of data isn't your thing, feel free to skip to the next section—there will be a summary!

DAY 3 (MID WEEK 1)

12 midnight	Settle baby
12:30 am	Put baby to bed
12:40 am	Baby wakes crying. Settle and put to bed
12:50 am	Baby wakes crying (again, sheesh!)
1:00 am	Feed baby
1:20 am	Burp and settle baby
1:45 am	Put baby to bed
	[Parents get 30 min sleep]
2:15 am	Baby wakes crying. Settle and put to bed
2:30 am	Put baby to bed
2:35 am	Baby wakes crying. Feed baby some more
3:00 am	Baby stops drinking. Burp and settle baby
3:20 am	Put baby to bed
	[Parents get 25 min sleep]
3:45 am	Baby wakes crying. Settle and put to bed

4:00 am   Baby wakes crying. Settle and put to bed

4:10 am   Baby wakes crying.

4:15 am   Midwife looks after baby

[Parents get 45 min sleep – luxury!]

5:00 am   Baby is returned crying. Feed baby

5:45 am   Dad takes baby to the parent's lounge

[Mum gets shower, food & 1 hr sleep]

7:45 am   Mum feeds and rocks baby in the parent's
              lounge

[Dad gets shower, food & 1 hr sleep]

9:45 am   Feed baby

10:30 am   Burp and settle baby

10:40 am   Put baby to bed

[Parents get 5 min sleep]

10:45 am   Pediatrician visit. Baby & parents wake

11:00 am   Put baby to bed

11:05 am   Physiotherapist visit. Baby wakes

11:20 am   Put baby to bed

11:30 am   Baby wakes crying. Feed baby

11:35 am   Obstetrician visit

12:00 noon   Burp and settle baby

12:10 pm   baby cuddles!

12:40 pm   Put baby to bed

1:20 pm   Baby wakes crying. Feed baby

2:00 pm   Family visit

2:15 pm	Put baby to bed
3:00 pm	Lactation consultant visits. Feed baby
3:30 pm	Burp and settle baby
3:45 pm	Put baby to bed
4:00 pm	Baby wakes crying. Feed baby
4:30 pm	Family leave
4:35 pm	Settle baby
5:00 pm	Put baby to bed
5:40 pm	Bath baby
6:00 pm	Feed baby
6:40 pm	Burp and settle baby
6:50 pm	Put baby to bed
6:55 pm	Baby wakes crying. Feed baby
7:10 pm	Burp and settle baby
7:15 pm	Put baby to bed
7:30 pm	Baby wakes crying. Feed baby
7:45 pm	Burp and settle baby
7:55 pm	Put baby to bed
9:00 pm	Baby wakes crying. Feed baby
9:20 pm	Burp and settle baby
9:25 pm	Put baby to bed
	[Parents get 25 min sleep]
9:50 pm	Baby wakes crying. Feed baby
10:10 pm	Burp and settle baby
10:20 pm	Put baby to bed

[Parents get 20 min sleep]

10:40 pm	Baby wakes crying. Feed baby
11:00 pm	Burp and settle baby
11:30 pm	Put baby to bed

[Parents get 30 min sleep]

12 midnight   Baby wakes crying. Feed baby

Baby cumulative sleep = 11–12 hours
Parent max. cumulative sleep = 4 hours

Interestingly, the first night with a baby is often quite calm and relaxed. The baby has just arrived into this world, and both mum and bub are exhausted. Day 2 is where the mayhem begins, as babies realize that everything around them is actually rather scary. Their food isn't on automatic supply anymore, so they start to get hungry.

On Day 2, many babies cry a lot and feed frequently (this is called cluster feeding, which will be discussed in another chapter). By Day 3, both baby and parents are exhausted, and four hours sleep is far from enough.

Note when looking at our Day 3 breakdown that we were in the thick of cluster feeding before Kate's milk supply had 'come in.' Parental sleep estimates assume that we fell asleep immediately after the baby did. Sometimes this did happen, because we were exhausted, but not always.

The schedule for Day 10 follows—again, if you aren't into numbers, feel free to skip to the next section.

DAY 10 (MID WEEK 2)

12:35 am	Baby wakes crying. Feed baby
1:55 am	Dad rocks baby to sleep in arms
	[Mum gets get 1 hr, 35 min sleep]
3:30 am	Feed baby from first breast[c]
	[Dad gets 25 min sleep]
3:55 am	Diaper change[d] & burp
4:10 am	Feed baby from other breast
	[Dad gets 30 min sleep]
4:40 am	Dad rocks baby to sleep in arms
	[Mum gets 1hr, 50 min sleep]
6:30 am	Baby wakes crying. Feed from first breast
	[Dad gets 30 min sleep]
7:00 am	Diaper change & burp
7:15 am	Feed baby from other breast
	[Dad gets 25 min sleep]
7:40 am	Dad rocks baby to sleep in arms

---

[c] *At this stage, a full feed involved the baby feeding from both breasts with a diaper change and burp in the middle.*

[d] *Because our child was born via cesarean, the mother had difficulty lifting the baby, meaning the father had to wake for all diaper changes.*

9:30 am	Baby wakes
10:00 am	Feed, burp and change baby's diaper
10:50 am	Mum rocks baby to sleep in arms

[Dad gets 1 hr, 10 min sleep]

12:00 noon	Diaper change
1:00 pm	Feed, burp and change baby's diaper
1:00 pm	Visitors arrive
1:40 pm	Baby sleeps
3:00 pm	Visitors leave
3:30 pm	Baby wakes crying. Feed and burp baby
4:30 pm	Bath baby
5:30 pm	Put baby to bed

[Parents get 1hr, 40 min sleep]

7:10 pm	Baby wakes
7:15 pm	Feed, burp and change baby's diaper
8:10 pm	Settle baby
8:20 pm	Put baby to bed
8:30 pm	Mum and Dad eat dinner at the same time!!
9:00 pm	Baby wakes. Feed baby
10:20 pm	Put baby to bed

[Parents get 1hr, 40 min sleep]

Baby cumulative sleep = 12–13 hours
Parent max. cumulative sleep = 6–7 hours

Note when looking at Day 10 that both parents started sleeping independently of each other. With our baby often unsettled by sleeping in a cot, which meant sometimes only 20 minutes before she started screaming, one person rocking the child while the other slept became the best way all three of us could grab the sleep we required. Doing this meant that each adult could get a respectable cumulative sleep, though this wasn't as good as one straight block! At this stage of a baby's development, many parents feel like 'all they do is feed the baby, change nappies, and sleep.' It's almost impossible to get anything else done.

Also of interest are the diaper changes, which needed to be done during every feed, and at other times as well. Because our child was born via emergency cesarean, Kate had trouble bending, meaning Nick was still assisting with all diaper changes (as well as every time our child needed to be lifted in or out of her bassinet). This gives an added level of sleep complication to children born by this method. Parents of children born vaginally may have more flexibility to protect the father's sleep, if they so choose, because the mother's body is affected differently.

This is something to keep in mind when thinking about family visits, caregivers and paternal leave if a family needs or chooses to have a cesarean—the mother will require a lot more care and help in the first six weeks until she recovers.

DAY 17 (MID WEEK 3)

12:05 am	Baby asleep after feed and diaper change
	[Parents get 50 min sleep]
12:55 am	Baby wakes, resettle
1:10 am	Baby goes back to sleep
	[Parents get 2 hrs, 41 min sleep]
3:51 am	Feed and burp baby
	[Dad gets 39 min sleep]
4:30 am	Diaper change
4:35 am	Dad rocks baby to sleep in arms
	[Mum gets 1 hr, 15 min sleep]
5:50 am	Feed, burp and change baby's diaper
7:20 am	Put baby to bed
	[Parents get 30 min sleep]
7:50 am	Baby wakes
8:20 am	Feed, burp and change baby's diaper
9:40 am	Settle baby
10:00 am	Put baby to bed
10:40 am	Baby wakes, resettle
11:00 am	Baby wakes. Feed, burp and change diaper
11:39 am	Put baby to bed

12:25 pm	Baby wakes, rock to sleep in arms
2:30 pm	Feed, burp and change baby's diaper
3:50 pm	Settle baby
4:00 pm	Put baby to bed
5:00 pm	Feed, burp and change baby's diaper
6:05 pm	Settle baby
6:15 pm	Put baby to bed
8:50 pm	Feed, burp and change baby's diaper
9:45 pm	Settle baby
10:45 pm	Put baby to bed (settling took some time)
11:02 pm	Baby wakes
11:08 pm	Feed baby from first breast
	[Dad gets 20 min sleep]
11:28 pm	Diaper change
11:35 pm	Feed baby from second breast

Baby cumulative sleep = 9-10 hours
Parent max. cumulative sleep = 5-6 hours

Note on Day 17 that though both parents and baby are technically getting less sleep than one week before, the patterns at which it occurs are slightly different. On Day 17, for the first time in almost three weeks, both parents got almost three hours sleep in one block. In these early days, this is the stuff that dreams are made of!

Week 3 saw some interesting developments in our child's sleep and feeding habits, and a pediatrician or mid-wife looking at this chart might see some unusual occur-rences. Feeding times for our child took up to 1 hour 20 minutes, which is much longer than average (breastfeed-ing sessions for newborns take on average 20-45 minutes).[12] Kate may be a doctor, but she was still a first time parent—a visit to the lactation consultant a week later helped reduce this feeding time considerably.

Note too, that at week 3 we were still having trouble getting our baby to sleep without being held. Shortly after this, we purchased a co-sleeping cot and our life (and sleep) suddenly changed. Co-sleeping cots are 'mini beds' which clip onto the side of the parent's bed, allowing par-ent and child to sleep together while creating a safe sleep surface for the child.[e]

Within touch and smell distance of her mother, our child settled much more rapidly. Combined with the use of a sleep suit, she started sleeping much better—the moral of this story is that if something doesn't work, ex-periment!

---

[e] *You can find more on safe co-sleeping practices at https://six-weeks.com/links/#5*

TLDR: ALL THOSE NUMBERS WERE BORING. I SKIPPED THEM

Honestly, we can't blame you. Many people reading this book will probably do the same, because let's face it—those columns of data were kinda long, and almost never ending…

Which is exactly the point.

The sleep deprivation never stops. You never get a break. Anyone can do one night of interrupted sleep. Most people can even do two or three late nights back-to-back. But thirty? Fifty? *One hundred* nights straight?

That can break you, if you're not expecting it.

Babies sleep in stops and starts, not one huge block. That means parents do too, and in these early weeks, you may feel like you never get enough time to sleep properly. Babies wake for a number of reasons—hunger, dirty nappies, hot or cold temperature, wind pain, or just for a comfort cuddle. It's our job as parents to be there for them because they can't look after themselves. This can be enormously tough on the parents.

HOW THIS APPLIES TO YOU

Children are not robots. They don't come pre-programmed with specific sleeping schedules. The timings above *will not* reflect exactly what your child does. So don't go setting stopwatches and thinking something is wrong if your child sleeps more or less than ours.

What you *should* take from this data is the spirit of the whole thing. The first six weeks are hard. You won't get much sleep—and hopefully now, you understand why.

WHEN DOES IT END?

The true definition of 'sleeping through the night' varies depending on which website you visit, but generally refers to uninterrupted sleep lasting anywhere between 3-8 hours for babies under the age of 6 months.[13] The maximum a one-day old baby will even be allowed to sleep at one time is four hours, including a feed (it's because they need to feed that they aren't allowed to sleep longer). In truth, they'll probably sleep for shorter periods than this anyway.

For some lucky parents, sleep is never a problem. They have a couple of hard weeks and then before they know it, their child is sleeping through the night (which, it should be noted, is something of a variable figure from parent to parent. Those without children often assume the phrase to mean 8-9 hours, but more often it will mean a stretch of time which is much shorter).

Others are still having sleep issues as their child becomes a toddler, or beyond. Put simply, there's no way to know how sleep will affect your child, or your family.

That said, medical professionals suggest that babies have the potential to be able to sleep through the night from around three months of age, or when they weigh 12 to 13 pounds (over 5 kilograms). That doesn't mean they *will*. It just means there's potential. Sleep hygiene—that is, good sleep practices for your child, such as a regular routine, can start much earlier.

About two-thirds of babies are able to sleep through the night on a regular basis by six months of age.[14] If you're struggling with it all, this is the age where you can hire a sleep professional or get out those sleep training books and start to do something about it.

So… take heart. While it's happening, lack of sleep can feel like a never-ending issue. But it *does* get better, slowly. There are going to be nights where you wake every 30 minutes, then every two hours, then every three. And then before you know it you'll be one of those parents looking back at your child's sleep history and thinking 'it wasn't such a big deal' too!

In the meantime, get assistance if you need it. Parents, grandparents, neighbors, friends and distant relatives are all great places to start—even if all they do is take your child as soon as you've fed them so your sleep is maximized while they do the burping and settling. When you're ready, sleep training will be possible, but it will take time for a child to grow and develop before this is an option.

For more information, check out the sleep training chapter, next.

6 | SLEEP TRAINING

Have you ever seen an amateur boxer get absolutely pummeled in the ring? Before the fight they're all cocky, jumping on the spot and punching the air. They have a plan, you see. They'll follow the coach's strategy and it will all be over in a heartbeat.

Here's the thing, though. Everyone has a plan until they get hit. After that, it's all just instinct. Maybe the boxer will win. Or maybe with that first punch they'll just collapse in a heap.

That's what sleep training is like. Everyone goes in with a plan. And that plan will work, guaranteed! But you never really know how you as a parent will hold up to the jab-and-uppercut combo of your child's screaming.

Me? I fell in a heap.

JAMES, FATHER OF ALINTA

Considering the sleep deprivation discussed in the previous chapter, it's no wonder the words 'Sleep Training' are a hot topic within the parenting community. Trust us, when your baby wakes at 3am in the morning only moments after putting him down, you'll do bleary-eyed research too.

The idea of sleep training is pretty self-explanatory—a variety of experts believe that techniques exist which will help your baby fall asleep faster and sleep longer, all without having to rock or hold them before they're put down.

First up, it is important to note that it *may* be a sign of health concerns if a child is overly sleepy in the first few weeks. You should check with your doctor if your child's desire to sleep is interfering with their feeding (a fasting time of more than six hours should be medically supervised).

Now that's said, can sleep training work? Yes and no.

'Yes' because all the experts agree that sleep training *does* work. And 'No' because in the first six weeks, most of these same experts believe a child is too young to start sleep *training*. Good sleep *hygiene* is still possible though, and you may be able to start sleep training shortly after. There are things you can do that may help lengthen the period of sleep an infant has, but there aren't any guarantees.

This is important to remember, because often the parents of older children misremember their own experiences (see our discussion on *oxytocin* in a previous chapter). Being told by someone that their child slept 'through the night' from the get-go (when chances are they didn't) and that your child should be able to as well (when each child is unique) sets false expectations and puts unrealistic pressure on new parents and babies.

Teaching a child how to sleep during the day poses similar issues during the first six weeks. Your infant will sleep a lot, but as you've seen in the chapter titled Sleepless Nights, it will most likely be in short, quick bursts. Good 'sleep hygiene' will be important here as the goal for daytime sleeping isn't to get a child to sleep for 6-8 hours straight, but rather to give them the energy to feed and have awake periods where they can develop and learn.

SLEEP HYGIENE DURING THE FIRST SIX WEEKS

Though many of the sleep training techniques that you'll read about in books and online aren't going to work in the first six weeks, there are a couple of great 'sleep hygiene' tips that can help for both day and nighttime sleeping.

Dr. Harvey Karp, a noted child sleep expert and pediatrician, advises that if your child falls asleep in your

Sleep Hygiene, Sleep Training & Self Settling

Think of *sleep hygiene* as things you can do 'around your child' that will help them fall asleep. In the first six weeks, effective sleep hygiene seems to mainly revolve around mimicking sounds, smells and actions that the baby has experienced in the womb. For example, playing white noise or swaddling an infant.

Sleep training is the specific process of teaching a child how to fall asleep—it's less 'what you can do with the environment' and more 'what you can do with the child' which is why it's appropriate a little later in a child's development (you're teaching them something new, as opposed to just replicating something familiar). Examples of sleep training might include patting a child to sleep or letting them 'cry it out.'

Self-settling is a concept that refers to your baby's ability to fall asleep by settling themselves without any help from the parent. Sleep hygiene and sleep training can either help or hinder this—if you always rock your child to sleep, for example, it may become harder for them to fall asleep on their own because you've 'trained' them to only fall asleep in your arms.

arms, you should wake them for a few drowsy seconds each time you put them down in their cot. The theory is that they'll open their eyes just enough to associate going to sleep with already being in the cot, as opposed to someone's arms, which will let them fall asleep in the cot faster in the future.[15]

Tizzie Hall, the author of *Save our Sleep*, advocates swaddling a child and then providing him or her with a comforter (a child-safe piece of material, for example a square of muslin, that will allow the baby to still breathe if it covers their face) that has been put down the mother's top for a few hours so that it smells like her. The baby then associates the mother as being close even when distant, and therefore sleeps better.[16]

Note: Even though all of the pediatricians, sleep experts and midwives we've spoken to about comforters believe that when properly used they can be a useful, safe tool for settling young infants, it's important to know that the SIDS guidelines (which you'll read about in a later chapter) for safe infant sleeping recommend against putting any loose articles in a child's bassinet, including comforters.

A work-around is to sleep with the bassinet's fitted sheet in your own bed prior to putting it in your child's.

This transfers a familiar smell to the infant's bassinet in a safe, SIDS compliant way.

When your child reaches six weeks of age, a few more options to help sleeping open up. On the Purple Crying website, Professor Ian St James-Roberts, a professor of child psychology, lists three things that have been found across multiple studies to be effective in managing infant sleep: [17]

1. Put your child down when they're sleepy but awake and avoid feeding or cuddling them to sleep (note that this is similar to Dr. Karp's recommendation).

2. Reduce light and interaction at night—for example, don't talk to your child when you change the nappy.

3. Once the baby is healthy, putting on weight and developing normally, delay feeding for a few moments when the baby wakes at night. The short delay means that waking isn't immediately rewarded by feeding. Do this gradually (use diaper changing to add a short delay if you want!) but don't leave the baby to cry for a long time.

SLEEP TRAINING AFTER THE FIRST SIX WEEKS

Professional bodies such as the Raising Children Network tell us that the average child isn't developmentally ready for independent sleep (that is, sleeping for 6-8 hours during the night, with the ability to fall back asleep without help if they wake) until six months or older.[18]

A baby *might* sleep through the night before this, they tell us, but if it happens it's due to the baby's personality, not something the parents are doing above and beyond providing an environment with 'good sleep hygiene.'

However there are many baby sleep experts who disagree. These people make claims (which it is important to note are not backed by research, but instead only by personal experience) that children can be taught months earlier.

Multiple books and courses state they can get children sleeping through the night sometime between six weeks and three months of age. None of the programs are instant, but rather rely on teaching your baby (and you!) good habits over time. Several are listed in the *Further Information* section at the end of this chapter.

Be aware that many sleep training books tend to assume a 'one size fits all' mentality—and babies come in lots of shapes and sizes! We've seen babies successfully sleep trained using the books and apps in our further information section, but that doesn't mean *any* program will work for *every* baby.

If you'd like to take a more personal approach, sleep consultants and sleep physicians are something to consider. Whereas books and apps can only give general advice, experienced professionals can tailor advice to *your* situation.

Sleep inpatient facilities, sometimes called 'sleep schools' or 'sleep centers,' are also worth investigating. These hidden gems (new parents rarely seem to know about them) usually involve a carer and their child staying at the facility through several sleep cycles—either across a full day, or overnight—so the child's sleep can be monitored and the parents coached. It may be worth asking your hospital or physician if there are any in your area!

CONTROLLED CRYING

Controlled crying is a contentious concept in the parenting world, and you'll often hear the words used as an expletive. Put simply, this sleep training technique revolves around a parent resisting the urge to pick up their child when she cries at the time she's laid to sleep. Instead, they wait for a short interval of minutes with the idea that when they don't rush over, the child will learn to settle themselves instead. If a parent can get it to work, it means the child will no longer rely on the parent to help them get to sleep (meaning more sleep for the adult, as well).

One of the reasons that emotions run so high on this issue, is... well... emotions. It's a heartbreaking thing to hear your child cry. It feels absolutely rotten to stand back and withhold comfort—surely that means its bad, right?

Thankfully, a lot of research has been done on this issue, though it takes some wading through online opinion pieces to find it. And there's a clear answer. While some researchers claim controlled crying in children may lead to post-traumatic stress in adulthood,[19] studies of the actual data suggest the worst that may happen is an increase in a child's stress levels for several days after the technique is used.[20] The child is crying because they want attention, not because they're in pain. Behavioral sleep techniques have no marked long-lasting effects on a child, either positive or negative.[21]

Put another way—if a baby is left to cry for a few minutes to help them sleep better but given love and affection for the other 23+ hours in a day, it's hard to imagine them suffering long term emotional damage.

So, controlled crying is something that you can choose to use (or not use!) for your family when your baby is old enough.

Unfortunately, as discussed earlier in this chapter, this will not be in the first few weeks.

If your baby becomes distressed during this period, you need to comfort them. When they're older, if they continue to have sleep issues, your own parenting style will help determine how you feel on this matter.

FURTHER INFORMATION:

Newborns: sleep, settling & routines (Website)
+ S*olving baby sleep problems (Website)*
The comprehensive, research-based articles on the *Raising Children* website are an excellent place to read more about sleep issues. Information includes how to settle a baby and how to change their sleep patterns.

Little Ones (App)
One of our favorite infant sleep programs, Little Ones is an app and website designed around using daytime feed and nap windows to get your baby sleeping better

overnight. The newborn program teaches parents the sleep hygiene required to get their baby sleeping for longer stretches overnight, while 3+ month programs establish routines that teach a baby to self-settle without fuss or crying.

Twelve Hours Sleep by Twelve Weeks Old (Book)
A short book with a name that says it all—Suzy Giordano believes that she can get any baby sleeping through the night (with no nighttime feeds) by three months of age. Serious sleep training starts at around four to six weeks of age, with the time before this spent focusing on preventing bad habits, (such as using vibration settings on rockers) that may limit success later.

Save our Sleep (Book)
Parents often have strong opinions about the routine-based sleep and feed schedules this book advocates, either loving or hating them. The book starts sleep training almost immediately after birth, relying on a 10pm dream feed (where a baby isn't woken fully before feeding) to get healthy infants sleeping through the night from the age of

four weeks. Dream feeds didn't work for us personally but have been successful for other families.

The Happiest Baby Guide to Great Sleep (Book)
Intelligent, practical advice on how to get your child to sleep better from a qualified pediatrician, with chapters for dealing with newborns all the way up to toddlers. There's no 'program' as such in this book, and no guarantee to have your child sleeping 12 hours by any age—just advice that any parent can use to stretch sleep periods out—so, great for parents who don't want to follow a routine.

Please see https://six-weeks.com/links#6 for web links.

7 | HOW TO CALM A CRYING BABY

Someone once told me they used to play recordings of crying babies to political prisoners as a torture technique. After listening to my child scream I can believe it. When it goes on long enough, you'll do anything—anything—to stop it.

KAREN, MOTHER OF AARIA

A baby's cry is one of the most distressing sounds in the world. And no wonder—scientists have found that our brains are hard-wired to respond, making us more attentive and priming our bodies to help whenever we hear it— even if we're not the baby's parents.[22]

Sometimes, to be honest, it's bloody annoying. Kate still bursts into tears when she hears a newborn crying over the back fence. But, it's not like babies can help it. In the first six weeks, it's one of the only sounds they can make. They'll use it to communicate how they're feeling, and that message is always important.

That's not to say that every time a baby cries, a new parent needs to panic! Yes, sometimes when a baby cries something can be seriously wrong, for example the child has been hurt or is unwell. But other times, it may just mean they're tired, or asking for comfort, or this 'whole new world' they're experiencing for the first time is a little overwhelming. And, sometimes babies just cry.

CHECK PHYSICAL REASONS FIRST

To calm a crying child, you should check the physical reasons that they might be upset first as these are all things that will have an immediate effect on their temperament. In order:

Hunger

If it's been a long time since your baby last fed (relative to the time period you usually feed them) your baby might be hungry. Look for 'mouthing' on your child, which can be small bubbles being blown in the saliva, sucking motions with the lips and tongue, or the child bobbing their head from side to side.

Diaper

Check for a dirty diaper if the baby is crying, and every time a baby feeds. No baby ever died from sitting in poo for an hour, but they do hate that cold, wet feeling.

Temperature

A general rule of thumb for infants is to dress them just a little warmer than you would yourself, usually described as 'whatever you wear, plus one layer'. If you're comfortable in a t-shirt, put them in a t-shirt *plus* a light sweater or wrap. If you're wearing a jacket, make sure they're even more warmly-dressed with an extra layer (for example, a singlet or undershirt beneath their top and sweater).

A baby is much more likely to cry if they are cold than if they are hot (hot babies get lethargic) but either extreme is dangerous. The easiest way to check is by feeling the nape of the neck to see if it's sweaty or cold to the touch (don't check the hands or feet as this can be misleading).

Is Your Child Unwell?

Use your common sense here. If something seems off, or greatly different from your baby's normal constitution, you should get it checked out—this may be the reason they're crying. You can also take their temperature—feel the back of the neck first, and if it seems hotter than it should be even with correct clothing and room temperature, grab a thermometer and see the chapter on sickness for more details.

> ### Tip: Pants off time
>
> Give your child some 'pants off' time every day so that their skin can air out away from the moist environment of a diaper. It doesn't have to be for a long period of time, even just five minutes lying on a blanket as you play with them (make sure the room is at an appropriate temperature!). It will help prevent painful diaper rash and keep your child happy.

EMOTIONAL REASONS

There's a good chance you'll get to the end of the Physical list and your baby will still be crying. It's your baby's call for comfort, and sometimes all they want is a cuddle. You can't "spoil" a newborn with too much attention, so don't hesitate to pick them up.

If holding them doesn't work, the good news is that there are other proven techniques which may help calm your baby.

One of the best is the 'Five S' technique by Dr. Harvey Karp, pediatrician and author of *The Happiest Baby*. It's based on the idea of mimicking the conditions in the womb as closely as possible. It makes sense that if a mother carried, rocked and fed her child in this environment for nine months, the child will take comfort in a similar environment once outside. Especially if you subscribe to the idea of the fourth trimester.

Dr. Karp's explanation of the 'Five S' calming technique[f] is reproduced here with permission:

The 1st S: Swaddle

Swaddling recreates the snug packaging inside the womb and is the cornerstone of calming. It decreases startling and increases sleep. And, wrapped babies respond faster to the other 4 S's and stay soothed longer because their arms can't wriggle around. To swaddle correctly, wrap arms snug—straight at the side—but let the hips be loose and flexed. Use a large square blanket, but don't overheat, cover your baby's head or allow unraveling.

Note: Babies shouldn't be swaddled all day, just during fussing and sleep, and should swaddling should be stopped at around two months (or whenever the baby begins to roll).

---

[f] *Please see https://six-weeks.com/links#7*

The 2nd S: Side or Stomach Position

The back is the only safe position for sleeping, but it's the worst position for calming fussiness. This S can be activated by holding a baby on her side, on her stomach or over your shoulder. Your baby should mellow in no time.

The 3rd S: Shush

Contrary to myth, babies don't need total silence to sleep. In the womb, the sound of the blood flow is a shush louder than a vacuum cleaner! But, not all white noise is created equal. Hissy fans and ocean sounds often fail because they lack the womb's rumbly quality. The best way to imitate these magic sounds is white noise.

A quick search will find a variety of white noise tracks for free online. Alternately, Dr. Karp sells a through his website,[g] and you can also find his white noise tracks for free on Spotify.

The 4th S: Swing

Life in the womb is very jiggly (Imagine your baby bopping around inside your belly when you jaunt down the stairs!). While slow rocking is fine for keeping quiet babies calm, you need to use fast, tiny motions to soothe a

---

[g] *Please see https://six-weeks.com/links#7*

crying infant mid-squawk. Dr. Karp's patients call this movement the "Jell-O head jiggle." To do it, always support the head and neck, keep your motions small; and move the body no more than 1 inch back and forth.

It's well worth watching Dr. Karp demonstrate the technique via his streaming video course, or on YouTube.[h] For the safety of your infant, never, ever shake your baby in anger or frustration.

The 5th S: Suck

Sucking is "the icing on the cake" of calming. Many fussy babies relax into a deep tranquility when they suck. Many babies calm easier with a pacifier.

The 5 S's Take PRACTICE to Perfect

The 5 S's technique only works when done exactly right. The calming reflex is just like the knee reflex: Hit one inch too high or low, and you'll get no response, but hit the knee exactly right and, presto!

Dr. Karp's *Happiest Baby* books are well worth checking out, and there's also a companion Streaming Video available on the website.[i]

---

[h] *Please see https://six-weeks.com/links#7*

[i] *Please see https://six-weeks.com/links#7*

Tip: Purple crying

Is your child still crying even after checking for physical reasons, and practicing the 5 S technique? Make sure you check the chapter on *purple crying*, next.

FURTHER INFORMATION:

The Happiest Baby on the Block (Book)
Advice on the changing sleep habits of children, including more further information on the 5S technique.

The Happiest Baby on the Block (Streaming Video)
Think of this as a streamlined version of the book—30 minutes long and just the essentials! It's a little cheesy, but if you look past that you'll find great advice.

How to wrap a baby (Video)
The title says it all—this video will show you step by step how to swaddle a baby and get them ready for sleep.

Please see https://six-weeks.com/links#7 for web links.

8 | P.U.R.P.L.E. CRYING, AKA COLIC

Colic is so hard to explain. When our baby cried everyone had advice, but what people just didn't understand was that nothing we did would stop Samir crying.

'Pick him up!' Auntie would say. 'Rock him. Stroke his face!'

'Yes,' we'd reply. 'But he will still cry.'

People thought we were being melodramatic, but we weren't. Sometimes when Samir cried, all he needed was a cuddle. Other times? Nothing we did could fix it.

I don't think we've ever fought as much as we did during that time. When you realize that all your strategies have failed your instincts kick in. And you can't get angry at the baby, so you get angry at each other. Nights in our house quickly devolved from 'the baby won't stop crying,' to 'the whole family won't stop crying.'

ADEBOWALE, FATHER OF SAMIR

Babies cry… a lot. But between the ages of 2 weeks and 3-4 months they may cry far more than many people expect, for hours at a time and for no apparent reason. Even just a couple of years ago, most doctors called this colic, however some experts are now also referring to this period as *purple crying*. In this chapter we'll use the terms interchangeably.

Colic (or purple crying) seems to affect some babies more than others. The old way of thinking about it was that a baby had colic if they experienced periods of inconsolable crying which lasted for more than three hours per day, more than three days per week, for longer than three weeks.[23] It's still a useful metric for abnormal crying volume or frequency.

'Colic' in this sense affects approximately 10% to 40% of infants worldwide. It peaks at around six weeks of age, with symptoms resolving by the time the child is three to six months old. [24]

The Period of Purple Crying is preferred by some doctors because the word 'colic' infers that there is something wrong with a baby, when there usually isn't—crying is distressing for all involved, but within a baby's development it's often very normal.

The Purple in *The Period of Purple Crying* is an acronym, which stands for:

Peak of crying

Your baby may cry more each week, the most in month 2, then less in months 3-5.

Unexpected:

Crying can come and go and you don't know why.

Resists Soothing:

Your baby may not stop crying no matter what you try.

Pain-like Face:

A crying baby may look like they are in pain, even when they are not.

Long Lasting:

Crying can last as much as 5 hours a day, or more.

Evening:

Your baby may cry more in the late afternoon and evening.

The word **Period** means that the crying has a beginning and an end.[25]

When your baby first starts crying inconsolably, make a visit to your local doctor, just to be sure everything is okay, but don't expect them to have a miracle cure. Purple crying / colic isn't something doctors are able to fix, but rather something that parents must endure.

WHAT CAUSES PURPLE CRYING?

There's an old wives' tale that gas causes colic, however this seems to be a symptom rather than a cause, as babies often swallow air when they cry. No one actually knows what causes purple crying, although contributing factors may include:[26]

- An immature nervous system, or unusually high sensitivity to stimulation
- Something the mother is eating
- Intolerance to formula ingredients (this is rare)

There's not much you can do about an immature nervous system—remember, babies are growing at an amazing rate! They may just be feeling things that they can't yet communicate other than by crying.

However, after visiting your pediatrician or primary care physician to ensure your baby doesn't have more serious issues, you can start experimenting with diet. First, if the infant is breastfed, the mother could try giving up cow's milk. One study suggests this may be beneficial in some infants (in the study, researchers put 66 mothers on a cow's milk free diet. Colic symptoms disappeared in 35 of the babies).[27]

Many people consume both coffee and chocolate whilst breastfeeding. We're not saying that everyone should avoid this, but if your infant is experiencing purple crying then it's worth trying. Caffeine (found in both coffee and chocolate) is transferred through breastmilk and is hard for a baby's body to break down, and as a result can slowly build up in their system. Some breastfeeding moms avoid eating broccoli, cabbage, beans, and other gas-producing foods as well. Research *has not shown* that these foods have a negative effect on babies,[28] but hey, there's no harm in trying as long as you're still eating other vegetables as part of a balanced diet.

Formula fed babies may also be sensitive to the milk protein in formula, though as mentioned above this is uncommon.[29] Talk to your physician if you think this is an issue. If food sensitivity is causing the discomfort, the colic should decrease within a few days.

Remember, all these ideas are just suggestions, and there's no guarantee they will work—if they did, purple crying wouldn't be that big of an issue! Many parents try everything they can to help their babies, and sometimes nothing works. If that happens to you, remember—it's unpleasant, but it's normal. And it won't last forever.

WHY ALL THE FUSS OVER A LITTLE CRYING?

Everyone wonders 'what's the big deal' before they have their first child, because we've all heard other babies cry and been able to ignore it. But a baby crying isn't just frustrating—it can be a real danger to a parent's mental fortitude, and therefore a baby's safety.[30] So, let's try to put this in perspective with a little story:

Imagine for a moment that the person you love most—perhaps the person you're having your child with—just suddenly started screaming. Like, really *shrieking*—those high-pitched cries that bounce around your brain. You'd drop everything and run to them, right? Because you knew they were being hurt, and in danger!

And now what if they just kept screaming? You search for danger but can't find any. They obviously haven't been injured, though they sound like it! You check every inch of their body but there are no rashes or bites, so you call the doctor. They can't find anything either.

And still this loved one screams and screams. Until they suddenly stop.

Blinking in surprise, you breathe a sigh of relief, asking them what's wrong. They look at you and shrug—then continue as if nothing had happened.

"Weird..." you mutter. You push it from your mind, until the next day, when you're both in an elevator and your loved one starts to scream again. Rounding on them, you tell them to cut it out. They're obviously not being hurt, so they must just be over-reacting. They ignore you and scream on.

You shake your head, then stumble as the elevator grinds to a halt. A light starts blinking on a control panel. The elevator is stuck.

Oh no. You put your hands over your ears. You shout for help. But your friend just screams and screams and screams, until hours later, as you're lying curled on the floor, suddenly they stop.

A buzzer goes off on the control panel. It's the fire warden, telling you there's been a problem. They can lower in food, blankets and a bucket, but it will take days to get you out. You shudder, looking at the person you love most and sob, waiting for tomorrow.

You're in the elevator for... you don't know how long. Each time you buzz the warden, he can't get you an estimate for when they'll have your problem fixed. And each day, at 3pm, your friend becomes a screaming monster. They. Just. Won't. Shut. Up.

The shrieks are piercing your brain, and you can't get out the door, and there's not even anything wrong! No matter how much you try and soothe them, or eventually burst out and yell at them, your loved one just ignores you. And continues to scream on and on and on.

Until suddenly the elevator doors scrape open, and you stumble blinking into the light. Just as you do, your friend stops screaming. They have a laugh with the rescue workers, and you know your ordeal has stopped.

That's what purple crying is like—equal measures heartbreaking and infuriating, made worse because there's nothing you can do, and you can't get away, *and you don't know when it will stop.*

As your child's guardian, it will test your mental and physical strength to the limits. And though you know how bad shaking your baby is, and that you'd never do it... sometimes, just sometimes, the crying gets so bad that you imagine what shaking your child just to have a moment's peace might be like...

STEP AWAY FROM THE BABY

Babies can be frustrating; bundles of joy one minute and screaming dervishes the next. As a parent, you'll be attuned to your own infant's cry, and when they're screaming, it can cause you distress.

Sometimes this distress turns to anger when nothing stops the crying. When that happens (and it will—it happens to even the best of us), just put the baby down and step away. Hand them to another caregiver if you can, or lay them down somewhere safe, step outside the door and take a deep breath.

Splash yourself with water, phone a friend or shut yourself in your bedroom and scream at the top of your lungs. Do whatever you must to calm down. But never, ever shake your child, even just a little bit, to quieten them. Their brains are so young and fragile that enormous injury can and has been done by parents, and the child could be damaged for life.[31]

SO, IT'S NORMAL. IS THERE ANYTHING I CAN DO?

Yes! This book has an entire chapter on calming crying children—if you skipped ahead, it's well worth a read! But for now, the important thing to remember is that if this happens to you it is normal, and it will stop. Batten down the hatches, get help and if you can, get some time away from your child every once in a while.

FURTHER INFORMATION

The Period of Purple Crying (Website)
Developed by a non-profit organization, this website is the original source of much of the information surrounding purple crying. It has suggestions on how to get children to sleep, how to soothe them and lots of resources for tired parents dealing with crying and fussy infants.

Colic Relief Tips for Parents (Web Article)
Developed by the AAP (American Academy of Pediatrics) the Healthy Children website is a great source of information on many things baby related. This particular page has a short but good list of recommendations for parents to help calm children during this difficult period.

Newborns: Crying & Colic (Web Articles)

Developed in conjunction with the Royal Children's Hospital Melbourne, the *Raising Children* website has a series of excellent articles and videos on colic, including information for dads, a video guide to baby cues, and picture-based instructions on how to soothe a child.

Please see https://six-weeks.com/links#8 for web links.

9 | UNDERSTANDING YOUR CHILD'S CRIES

It's amazing to me that we can become so in tune with our little ones that we understand them when no-one else does. Even the cries soon make sense. Whereas a stranger will just hear one long wail, I'll hear 'I want my diaper changed,' or 'please burp me, I have wind.' It's like our own private little language.

SOFIA, MOTHER OF ALEJANDRO

Did you know your child can communicate with you from the moment they're born? It's possible for new parents to recognize and interpret their infant's cries, and therefore understand what their baby wants long before they can talk.

The theory in a nutshell is that very young children, across all cultures, make the same five sounds when they want or are experiencing specific things. The hypothesis was developed by Australian former mezzo-soprano singer Priscilla Dunstan and gained popularity after being featured on The Oprah Winfrey Show.

The theory may initially sound crazy, but after careful thought starts to make more sense—sound is shaped by the position of the tongue, mouth, lips and body. The sounds aren't intentional, but if a baby is hungry it will try to suck, moving its lips and tongue to a very different position than if it has wind, or is tired.

WORDS (SOUND REFLEXES)

According to Dunstan, the five universal words (or sound reflexes) used by infants are:[32]

Neh (I'm hungry)

An infant uses the sound reflex "Neh" to communicate its hunger. The sound is produced when the sucking reflex is triggered, and the tongue is pushed up on the roof of the mouth.

Owh (I'm sleepy)

An infant uses the sound reflex "Owh" to communicate its tiredness. The sound is produced like an audible yawn.

Heh (I'm experiencing discomfort)

An infant uses the sound reflex "Heh" to communicate stress, discomfort, or perhaps the need for a fresh diaper. The sound is produced by a response to a skin reflex, such as feeling sweat or itchiness in the bottom.

Eairh (I have lower gas)

Infants uses the sound reflex "Eairh" to communicate that they have flatulence or an upset stomach. The sound is produced when trapped air from a belch is unable to release and travels to the stomach where the muscles of the intestines tighten to force the air bubble out. Often, this sound will indicate that a bowel movement is in progress, and the infant will bend its knees, bringing the legs toward the torso. This leg movement assists in the ongoing process.

Eh (I need to be burped)

An infant uses the sound reflex "Eh" to communicate that it needs to be burped. The sound is produced when a large bubble of trapped air is caught in the chest, and the reflex is trying to release this out of the mouth.

It's important to understand that Dunstan's ideas have not been scientifically validated. That is, there are no major studies proving one way or the other if her ideas work beyond her own inhouse research.[33] But a quick google will unearth hundreds of appreciative parents who swear by the method's effectiveness.

We experimented with Dunstan Baby Language with our own child. Though to us the cries perhaps weren't as clear as we expected (it takes effort and concentration to spot the differences sometimes!), they were definitely there and of great help in the first few days deciphering if our child needed a diaper change, to feed or be burped.

If you'd like to practice learning the five sounds, we'd suggest *actually listening* to the sounds instead of just reading the descriptions above. What on earth does 'eairh' sound like, for example, when you're trying to pronounce it?

The Dunstan Baby Language website features a number of courses new parents might be interested in, including online videos, a DVD collection and an app. Alternately, watching the Oprah Winfrey segment on YouTube is free, almost as good, and a great way to tell if you can hear the differences in a baby's cry as well!

Remember, some people can't hear any differences in their baby's cry as well. If that's you, don't stress! This technique is great if it works, but the world won't end if it doesn't.

FURTHER INFORMATION

Dunstan Baby Language (Website)
The original source of information about Priscilla Dunstan's theory of baby language.

Oprah Winfrey interview (YouTube Video)
The video is low quality but includes examples of baby sounds and their explanations... and you can't beat *free*. Perfect for those on a budget.

Please see https://six-weeks.com/links#9 for web links.

10 | ROOM TEMPERATURE

Room temperature isn't something I paid attention to before having a baby. I usually work on the rather vague Goldilocks principle of too hot, too cold or just right, and there's a fair bit of variance between the three depending on my mood and how much effort is required to open a window. But on the first night we brought our baby home I must have checked the temperature beside her crib every 10 minutes!

MARK, FATHER OF CONNIE

The optimal room temperature for a clothed child's comfort is between 68F - 72F (20C – 22C).[34] If you don't have a thermometer, judge the room's temperature by what feels comfortable to you.

A child won't explode if the room goes up or down by a degree, but over or under-heating your child can lead to serious problems, so it's best not to push the boundaries too far. Babies can wake up unnecessarily in cold conditions, and overheating can not only lead to fever, but is thought to increase the risk of sudden infant death syndrome (SIDS).[35]

When dressing a baby, the trick to the right amount of clothing, as mentioned in an earlier chapter, is to look at what you're wearing plus one.

Think layers—adding or removing them as necessary until the baby is comfortable. Pay particular attention when moving a newborn from outside to inside, and vice versa, as it's easy to dress a child for one environment, which then affects them when they move to another.

Investing in a room temperature monitor is a nice luxury if you can afford it, but not essential if you remain aware of your own surroundings.

FURTHER INFORMATION

The right temperature for a baby (Web Article)
A detailed rundown on what the right room temperature is for a baby, with a great question and answer section.

Please see https://six-weeks.com/links#10 for web links.

11 | SICKNESS

I always thought the first time I took my child to the emergency room would be in a flurry of tears and panic. Instead, we crept up to the counter, sheepish as heck and slightly embarrassed at three in the morning. "We're new at this," I explained, holding up my son. "I'm sorry if we're over-reacting."

My child had a temperature. It was only slightly higher than normal, but he wouldn't stop crying. And I had no idea what to do. Was a temperature more dangerous for an infant than an adult? The internet forums were full of conflicting information.

I felt even worse when we were admitted. I kept apologizing, because in the next room there was a person having a heart-attack and my baby just had a fever.

The emergency room attendants didn't care. "Babies are so fragile," they said. "You did the right thing."

We were home four hours later. Though our child was fine, I'm still glad we went to hospital—because I didn't know if my baby was okay, so it was important I ask.

You're not acting in your own interests in a situation like this—you're acting for a tiny little clone that isn't yet capable of looking after himself. It doesn't matter how you feel, or how embarrassed or how much self-doubt you have about whether you're over-reacting. You just do what's right for the baby. And if you don't know, that means asking the professionals.

KATHERINE, MOTHER OF NATE

The first (and sometimes *only*) sign of serious illness in many babies under three months will be a fever. A normal temperature in babies is between 36.5C - 38C (97.7F – 100.4F).[36] With infants, it's worth monitoring your child very closely (and possibly consulting a health professional) if their temperature rises above 37.4C (99.32F). Young children get really sick *very* fast.

If your baby is warmer than 38C (100.4F), even by a little bit, take them immediately to see a doctor.

To know if your child is too hot or too cold you'll need a thermometer. There are various kinds that you can purchase, including 'no touch' ones that you place near the forehead, and another that you insert in the anus (sheesh!).

While rectal thermometers are marginally more accurate,[37] our preference is for an *axillary* or *tympanic* thermometer (when your child is sick and finally falling asleep after three hours of screaming, the last thing you'll want to do is shove a cold plastic probe where the sun don't shine). Axillary thermometers measure the temperature beneath an armpit, while tympanic devices measure the temperature of the eardrum inside an ear. Tympanic devices are typically much faster but also more expensive, so it will be up to you and your budget as to which you choose.

Note that 'no touch' electronic thermometers that measure the temperature just above the forehead also exist but are not recommended for children under three months of age. Called temporal artery thermometers or forehead thermometers, their readings aren't accurate enough for infants. Old-style mercury thermometers aren't recommended either (they'll can potentially release poisonous vapors if dropped and shattered).

New parents are famous for being over-cautious about their babies. Stories abound of tired mothers and fathers rocking up to the emergency room only to be told that their child is fine. But… better this, than the opposite.

It pays to be cautious when you have an infant, as they are so small and tiny that things can go wrong fast. No medical professional will ever laugh at you for being concerned about your baby.

Beyond a temperature, here are a couple of things that you should look for:[38]

- 'The usual' symptoms of illness in adults (because many of these will be true for babies, too). This includes convulsions, excessive vomiting (babies do regurgitate, sometimes often, but they shouldn't be throwing up their entire meal), and rashes and purple splotches on their skin
- A baby obviously in pain, or shrieking inconsolably
- An awake baby that is listless or limp
- Not peeing/no wet nappies in several hours (especially in the first few weeks)
- Noticeable changes in feeding or a baby's usual behavior

This is not a complete list and shouldn't replace advice from your baby's doctor. Remember, if in doubt, check it out! Being worried about a healthy baby is better than the alternative.

You may feel you have no instincts for this if you're new, however remember even after a few weeks you will know your baby better than anyone. Doctors and nurses are the health experts, but you're the expert in *your baby*. If you feel something is well outside the normal range of expectations for your baby, trust that—it's just as sensitive a vital sign as anything else, and there's even research to prove it![39]

Tip: Parent Health

Babies aren't the only vulnerable people in your new family! Parents experience very real risks of becoming run down as they skip sleep, meals and exercise to care for their newborn baby. Don't be afraid to ask family, friends, neighbors and support groups for help if you think you need it.

FURTHER INFORMATION

Recognizing newborn illnesses (Web Article)
An easy-to-read list by the American Academy of Family Physicians of different types of newborn illnesses.

When to call a doctor (Web Article)

Another list, this time by the Seattle Children's Hospital. It gives typical symptoms of a sick infant, categorized by how urgently you need to call a doctor if you see them.

Newborns: Safety (Web Articles)

An easy to navigate series of pages on child safety covering such topics as poisons, pets, burns, water safety and CPR for infants. Funded by the Australian Government.

Please see https://six-weeks.com/links#11 for web links.

12 | BABY MAGIC

I can still remember the first time I lay my newborn on my bare chest. Hours old, eyes closed and barely sentient, her fingers wrapped around my thumb—with no awareness of anything else, she was still aware of our connection. She knew I was her daddy. That I was her entire world. In that moment, I swore I'd live up to the expectation.

MICHAEL, FATHER OF DAVINA

Did you know that if you lay your infant on your chest, their breathing will slow down or speed up to match your own? Or that your own body temperature will change to help regulate the baby's? It feels a little like magic! Skin-to-skin contact is a delightful, rewarding experience for both baby and caregivers (and that includes partners!).

Unable to self-regulate many of their basic biological functions, the bodies of newborns regulate heart rate, blood pressure, sleep cycles, skin temperature, and brain chemistry from close contact with the bodies of their parents.[40]

Skin-to-skin contact can start immediately after birth—in fact, the World Health Organisation considers it *so beneficial* that they recommend a newborn baby be placed on the mother's chest for the first hour after a baby is born![41] Many hospitals follow this practice, if they can, though sometimes other things become more important, such as looking after the health of the baby or mother. If you intend to have a cesarean, check the hospital's policy.

Later, performing skin-to-skin contact with the baby's father (or other caregiver) provides benefits for both the baby and adult. The baby's benefits include improvement in temperature and pain control, and behavioral responses, and for the carer there are improvements in establishing the role as 'parent' and in developing positive behaviors when interacting with the new baby.[42]

Skin-to-skin has also been found to help with breastfeeding, reduce baby crying (and parental stress!), and improve bonding.[43] It also aids preterm infant brain development[44] and helps colonize the baby with good bacteria already present on a parent's skin.[45] In other words, it really is important!

But 'baby magic' goes beyond just skin-to-skin. Parents tell numerous stories of their child 'sensing' their presence when they're close by—and often instantly calming! One friend recounts the story of trying to put their toddler to sleep each night, only to have them wake without fail each time the parent tried to sneak from the room.

With our daughter, we had a similar experience. When our new family was just one week old and returned from the hospital, we learned the hard way that our daughter sleeps best within touching distance of her mother.

Our infant is a noisy sleeper. As a loving father, Nick thought the best thing he could do for our situation was take our child from the room when she fell asleep so that she didn't disturb the exhausted mother. Kate slept well, but our little girl didn't!

When a midwife friend visited, she rolled her eyes when we explained the problem. "Newborns settle much better when they're close to their mother," she said. "Try putting her bassinet back in the room, right next to the bed." The first night we did it, our child jumped from half hour naps to sleeping an entire two hours.

Every child is of course different. The important thing is to play and experiment with what works for you within safe guidelines. But we're telling you right here and now, there's no denying it. Baby magic exists. And when you experience it, it's wonderful.

FURTHER INFORMATION:

Pure Love (YouTube Video)
A sweet, four-minute exploration of the power of skin-to-skin contact, which sees newborn baby heart rates monitored while swaddled and then held against their mother. *Aww...*

Keep Mother and Baby Together (Research Article)
A rather more scientific analysis of the benefits of skin-to-skin contact, as originally published in the Journal of Perinatal Education.

Evidence on skin-to-skin after cesarean (Web Article)
An article by the website Evidence Based Birth on the benefits and challenges of skin-to-skin contact

immediately after a cesarean. For the amount of data given and referenced, it's a surprisingly easy read.

Please see https://six-weeks.com/links#12 for web links.

13 | MOTHER'S MIND & BODY

When I had twins by cesarean I had problems recovering from the surgery—I was still in pain seven months later as they were starting to crawl. I couldn't pick up anything heavier than a baby... a problem when you don't just have one, but two.

I still remember the day I was trapped at a local park, unable to leave. I'd decided to let the twins (Liam & Noah) crawl around on the grass.

My problems started when it was time to go home. I picked up Liam, grunting in effort, only to see Noah take off like a four-limbed rocket! Putting Liam down I chased after his brother. It was only when I caught Noah that I realized my mistake—now Liam was speeding away lightning fast.

I began making my slow, painful way back, but had to put Noah down when his brother made a beeline for the road. By the time I caught him, carrying him back to safety, I turned to see Liam getting himself into trouble.

It was like they knew I could only carry one twin and were working together in their bid for freedom. Each time one was captured the other would do something dangerous, demanding I release the one I was holding.

It felt like this went on for hours. I'm almost certain I aged several years.

Eventually, a random stranger approached, swooping to pick one twin up. Normally this is something I wouldn't approve of. But when he said he'd noticed my predicament and wanted to help, I burst into grateful tears.

GRACE, MOTHER OF LIAM & NOAH

It takes nine months to cook a baby, and during that time a mother's body changes a lot. Hormones flood her as organs move and change, and skin stretches. After birth, it will take time to get things back to the pre-birth conditions most people expect.

Notice how we didn't say 'back to normal?' That's because all these changes *are* normal for after a birth. It's an important point to remember.

BODY

No-matter what the method of delivery, a mother's body undergoes trauma and will need time to recover after the birth of her child. Bleeding, constipation, fatigue, breast discomfort and stitches are normal, and women can face hemorrhoids and perineum discomfort, too.[46]

Recovery from vaginal birth can take several weeks if a woman doesn't tear, and over six weeks if she has a perineal tear or episiotomy. Women who have had a cesarean will spend several days in hospital being monitored before they are allowed home, and it will take another four to six weeks before they start feeling like they did before the surgery. After both types of delivery it can take many more weeks for the body to recover enough that exercise can be contemplated, and a check-up with a physiotherapist is advised before any sort of physical activity is started.

During this time, a lot of the physical workload will fall upon partners and other caregivers. After a c-section, for example, a woman's tummy will be sore—she's just had major abdominal surgery after all! It will be a struggle to rise from bed, and incredibly challenging to lean over a cot and lift a screaming baby. Caregivers will become just as physically exhausted as the mother, necessarily going through the same sleep deprivation experience of getting up every time the baby cries, needs a diaper change or feed, until the mother is fully recovered.

Getting back to pre-pregnancy shape will take time too! There's an old saying: "It took nine months for your body to get this way, let it have nine months to change back." Though its possible (and often advisable) to start your fitness regime much earlier, the sentiment not to expect too much too soon is worthwhile.

That said, the American College of Obstetricians and Gynecologists recommends that a woman start exercising 'as soon as she feels ready' and that for a vaginal birth with no complications, this can be within a couple of days.[47] Women who have had a cesarean birth or complications will take longer, and should talk to their health care provider.

Exercise should be gentle at first—for example walking your child around the block in their stroller. Movie stars with dedicated trainers, babysitters and personal chefs may be able to drop the pregnancy weight in six weeks, but the average for most 'normal' mothers is much, much longer. In these first weeks, don't be surprised if you still have a belly no-matter what you do! The uterus has to shrink back to pre-pregnancy size, and this can take around six weeks all on its own.

Finally, it's worth noting that some women experience hair loss after the birth of their child, which can be something of a shock. But don't worry, even though it might come out in large clumps! Your hair is most likely just returning to its normal state—during pregnancy, the hormones coursing through a mother's body makes her hair thicker and more luxurious. After pregnancy, as these hormones leave her body, that excess hair falls out. Most women see their hair return to its normal fullness by their child's first birthday. Many women regain normal fullness even earlier.[48]

But speaking of hormones…

HORMONES

When most people think about changes after birth, the physical stuff comes to mind pretty quickly, but the hormonal stuff… maybe not so much. Perhaps that's because many of the hormonal changes experienced affect mood and mental health—neither of which are as obvious to the onlooker as changes like weight gain. Or maybe it's just because people don't talk about it quite so much.

A woman's hormones can be problematic—not just for the new mother, but for the entire family. Baby Blues are often the most immediate and striking effect, frequently occurring within 2-3 days of delivery. Baby Blues are a period of intense emotional upheaval for a woman and can often be confusing because they come at such a happy time! Their cause may be linked to the hormonal fluxes occurring within the mother.

Some midwives advise that the best treatment for Baby Blues is to 'cry it out'—that tears are nature's way of flushing all those now excess hormones from a woman's body. While there's no scientific research to back the claim up, there is some merit to the advice. Many mothers say that they feel much better after putting on *Marley & Me* or *The Notebook* and just sobbing for a few hours.

Up to 80% of all mothers are affected by the Baby Blues, but the good news is they don't last long and they usually go away on their own.[49] Typically this happens several days after symptoms start, but they can sometimes last a couple of weeks. Medical experts we've spoken to often say that day three is the worst.

If the Baby Blues *don't* go away, a woman may be suffering from postpartum depression, also called postnatal depression. Affecting up to 15% of mothers (that's 1 in 7!), this is a much more serious condition that requires external help to resolve. The new mother's experiences can be extreme and may interfere with her ability to care for herself or her family. If a mother feels sad for more than two weeks, feels especially anxious, has feelings of shame, guilt, or considers hurting herself or her baby, she should seek professional treatment immediately.

With postpartum depression, it's important to understand that this *isn't the woman's fault*. For those predisposed to experience it there's little that can be done to avoid postpartum depression, and factors such as diabetes, high stress or previous abuse can exacerbate the symptoms. The important thing is to be on the lookout and to talk to someone if you think you're at risk.

Men experience postpartum depression too (in males, it's called paternal postpartum depression, or PPD). Up to 1 in 10 new fathers suffer from it, and while it may occur immediately after birth just like in women, it tends to be more common three-to-six months after the arrival of their child.[50] Women tend to turn their sadness and fear inward, but men are more likely to express depression through anger, aggressiveness, irritability and anxiety. Men with PPD are also susceptible to increased drinking, drugs, and addictive behaviors such as gambling or playing video games.[51]

Postpartum depression in men and women IS treatable. Everyone involved in the care of newborns should look out for it and talk about it if they think it's an issue. But again, treatment requires external help— if you can identify with any of the symptoms, see your GP or obstetrician as a first port of call. Sometimes all you need is a couple of chats with a therapist.

It's vital not to self-medicate, especially if a mother is breastfeeding, as some over-the-counter medicines are transferred through breastmilk and aren't safe for a baby. Prescription medications from doctors that know a mother is breastfeeding—and have considered this when choosing the most appropriate treatment—are safe for her to take.

Even if a woman isn't depressed, it's important to realize that her hormones will still be fluctuating wildly in the first six weeks after giving birth. They will slowly settle down, but mood swings can be common: a mother can be happily laughing one minute, and then sobbing the next. Hormones are still flooding her body, and sleepless nights don't help, either. This is tough not just for her, but also for her partner.

Couples can expect to have fights in these first few weeks, and big ones! No matter how synchronized you might believe yourselves to be before a baby is born, afterwards everyone will have a different opinion about the best way to care for their child, or stop it crying. Add to that a few sleepless nights and a healthy dose of fluctuating hormones and…well…just remember that you all love each other very much and that this phase in your lives will pass.

The important thing to remember is that the *tough times don't last forever*. For many people, the first six weeks with a new child are the absolute hardest period of their lives, but it does get better. Your baby will eventually sleep more and cry less. You will survive.

FURTHER INFORMATION:

(Mental Recovery)

Postpartum Depression in Women (Fact Sheet)
An excellent resource if you think you might be depressed, or are just curious about what the signs of postpartum depression are, in an easy to read article that talks about what depression is, what the risk factors are, and what treatment options are available.

Anxiety & Depression in Pregnancy & Early Parenthood (Fact Sheet)
This fact sheet addresses antenatal depression in both men and women, listing specific signs to look out for.

Postpartum Depression in Men is Real (Web Article)

An interesting read that follows one man's experience with paternal depression, from realizing something was wrong to doing something about it.

(Physical Recovery)

Your Body After the First 6 Weeks (Fact Sheet)

A list of questions and answers discussing common issues a mother may experience after birth, such as perineum soreness, swelling and constipation, and what can be done about it.

Postpartum Recovery Timeline (Web Article)

What a new mother can expect her physical and mental health to possibly look like on a week-by-week basis after birth, with handy charts and great suggestions for aiding recovery.

❖

When to Start Exercising After Birth (Fact Sheet)
A simple list of questions and answers by the American College of Obstetricians and Gynecologists discussing when and how a mother can get back into physical exercise.

Please see https://six-weeks.com/links#13 for web links.

14 | BREASTFEEDING: A LEARNED ART

I'm so tired of hearing that breastfeeding is the most natural thing in the world.

It's not. It's a skill—a learned skill.

Some mothers grasp this skill instinctively, I'm sure, just like some people can yodel or ride a bike without being taught. But the rest of us need singing lessons and training wheels, and someone correcting our mistakes so we don't get hurt.

HONEY, MOTHER TO AMY, BELLE & CELESTE

Before becoming pregnant most couples only know the basics about breastmilk. The baby arrives and the milk comes out... what more is there to know?

Well, as it turns out, quite a lot.

Breastfeeding may be natural, but it most certainly isn't easy. For many women, it can be a struggle they didn't expect. Perhaps our ancestors 10,000 years ago could just pop a child on the teat, but in this modern age breastfeeding is a learned art. It's worthwhile knowing— at the very least—a couple of important concepts so that the mother's breastfeeding experience, should she choose to do so, is as smooth as possible.

COLOSTRUM

Many new parents are surprised to discover that a mother's milk does not come instantly after birth. Generating an appropriate supply is an act of teamwork between mother and child, and the process is pretty ingenious.

When a baby is born, its stomach is only the size of a pea. They don't actually need a stomach in the womb (their mother's placenta supplies everything they need), so why waste all that space? Of course, as soon as they're born babies need to feed, and their stomach rapidly grows.

With the stomach so small, the baby's mother generates a special kind of milk in those first few days called *colostrum*. Think of it like royal jelly compared to regular honey—colostrum is a nutrient rich superfood for the baby that gives it the energy it needs until its stomach can grow large enough to hold an appropriate amount of milk. The breast may only give a couple of drops with each feed, but it contains so much of 'the good stuff' that it's enough. Mothers-to-be may notice colostrum beading on their nipples in the days leading up to birth. It can be clear, golden yellow or orange-y in color.

As the baby's stomach grows in those first few days, these couple of drops of colostrum become less and less satisfying. This leads to...

CLUSTER FEEDING

Our second important concept for new parents is the idea of cluster feeding, which is basically just the baby getting really, really hungry about 24-48 hours after birth and wanting to feed almost constantly. The child's stomach is growing, but the mother is still only producing drops of colostrum. The baby tries to feed much more frequently than in the first day, and this is an exhausting but important time for new parents.

Exhausting, because the feeding can be as frequent as every 20 minutes, and it can last for several days. The mother will get zero sleep as the child just sucks and sucks like a little newborn vacuum cleaner trying to get more and more liquid to satiate its hunger.

Important, because all this sucking has an incredible effect on a woman's body. It helps stimulate the breasts, stopping the production of colostrum and beginning the formation of breastmilk.

Cluster feeding occurs around one to two days after birth (usually in the evenings). It will occur again at around three weeks and then again at six weeks, as the baby goes through growth spurts and 'trains' the mother to produce more milk.

SUPPLY AND DEMAND

Breastfeeding is all about supply and demand. That is, the more a baby sucks on a breast, 'demanding' milk, the more a body produces—at least, for the first six weeks. After this, even as your child grows, the mother's milk volume will stay roughly the same (if she doesn't do anything to reduce it). So don't stress if your baby is happy but your milk supply isn't increasing as your child grows after the first six weeks, because it's not meant to.

OUR BREASTFEEDING JOURNEY

From the first moment we found out we were having a baby, Kate was keen to breastfeed. But having several very good friends who had experienced issues and knowing others who weren't physically able to breastfeed at all (due

Tip: Do a Class

Mothers: if you want to breastfeed, do a course *before* your child is born. Most countries have breastfeeding associations, and their advice can be invaluable.

There is sooo much more to breastfeeding than just putting a baby on a nipple. Breastfeeding courses not only provide practical advice on how to hold your child, care for your breasts and what to expect, but also help with everything from what to eat, to what to do when things go wrong!

La Leche League is a worldwide, non-profit organization that advocates breastfeeding, and a great place to start. Additionally, many countries also have individual organizations with support hotlines staffed by volunteers.

See https://six-weeks.com/links#14 for a list with more information!

to, for example, inverted nipples), she was keen to do a class so as to have 'more tools in the toolbelt' when we started feeding our own child.

And boy, are we glad we did! From dealing with mastitis and blocked milk ducts (an almost weekly experience for Kate) to troubleshooting breastfeeding problems, the class was incredibly useful. Whilst our initial experiences with breastfeeding were straightforward—our daughter latched from the first instant—having that extra knowledge to lean on when things took an unexpected turn was invaluable. And though our journey was certainly less complicated than some, it was still on occasion insanely hard, arduous, and frustrating. We had to navigate rapids that included nipple damage from prolonged feeds, poor milk supply after mastitis, breast pain and leaking nipples (wet patches on a shirt are sooo hot right now).

Breastfeeding was a steep learning curve! You'd think the whole process should be easy—pop a baby on, make sure they're sucking and *hey presto*, everyone's happy. Not so. As a doctor, Kate may know far more about the human body than an average person, but medical school never taught her how to position a baby *just right* across the chest so she sucks correctly, or even how to tell when a breast was full or empty (that one came from experience).

At the start, we were even feeding our child incorrectly, unwittingly tripling the time our child had to stay on the breast to gain the milk she required. We only realized our mistake (it's super important that dads and other carers be involved in breastfeeding too!) when we saw a lactation consultant for nipple damage—the consultant pointed out that our daughter was pulling and tugging on the nipple in frustration at the poor flow, and showed us how to feed correctly.

There's absolutely no shame in admitting that breast-feeding is physically and emotionally taxing. It takes a lot of work for many moms and babies to get right (and sometimes, no matter how hard a mother tries, it may be impossible as well). If you're keen to try and breastfeed, getting more information before your child is born will be an invaluable help afterward!

Our Breastfeeding Journey: Mastitis

Sometimes it feels like everyone has something go wrong. Some parents have to deal with colic and purple crying. Others have hormonal changes, or sleepless nights. We had *mastitis.*

An inflammation of the breast tissue, mastitis is excruciatingly painful. It's often caused by blocked milk ducts—the milk banked up behind the duct is forced into nearby breast tissue, causing it to become inflamed.[52] It can also be caused by bacterial infections when milk in a breast that isn't emptied becomes stagnant, providing a breeding ground for bacteria. Either way, the inflammation that results can cause breast pain, swelling, warmth and redness. It may also cause fever and chills.[53]

Early symptoms of mastitis can feel like you're getting the flu. Kate would get shivers and aches, which set in very quickly. Breasts also become red, sore, swollen, hot and painful.[54]

With mastitis, prevention is better than cure. Noticing and treating issues such as blocked ducts before they lead to mastitis can prevent the situation evolving into something worse. Take our word for it—try to avoid mastitis if you can. New mothers should make it standard practice after every feed to check both breasts for lumps and hard spots in the breast tissue, which may be a sign of milk 'backing up' behind a blocked duct.[55]

If you do notice that you have a blocked duct, La Leche League provides a series of ideas that mothers can try to clear it, including:[56]

- Apply wet or dry heat to the affected area
- Remove any dried milk secretions on your nipple by soaking with plain warm water
- Use gentle breast massage on any hard, lumpy areas while your baby feeds
- Try to feed your baby on the affected side frequently, in a variety of positions
- If possible, loosen constrictive clothing or go bra-less for a few days

Kate also found therapeutic ultrasound to be a highly effective method of combating blocked ducts. The technique, which involves using an ultrasound machine to generate sonar vibrations within the breast, seems rarely mentioned on breastfeeding websites but has been proven in studies[57] (and our own experience) to work.

If you don't have access to physiotherapists or other professionals able to use this technique, La Leche League suggests holding the flat end of a vibrating electric toothbrush against your breast.[58] We have friends who've used a vibrator to do the same thing in an emergency. *Ahem.*

Though her issue isn't common, in our situation Kate's blocked ducts seemed primarily caused by the presence of milk blisters on her nipples. These small, 'white' spots (they may also be pink or light yellow in color) are caused by either an overgrowth of skin over a milk pore, or a small amount of thickened milk.[59] Exactly as the name implies, these blisters-full-of-milk prevent the milk behind it from draining during a feed. The Australian Breastfeeding Association has an excellent resource page[j] on milk blisters (also called milk blebs) which contains photos to aid with identification and a list of at-home treatment options, including:[60]

---

[j] *Please see https://six-weeks.com/links#14*

- Ensuring the baby continues to feed from the affected area (suction may help break the fragile layer of skin over a white spot, or move thickened milk)
- Soaking the nipple in warm water and then rubbing it gently with a washcloth
- Massaging olive oil into the affected nipple

If the milk blister is resistant to these treatments, it's also possible to use a sterile needle to gently release the blockage. This is a delicate process best left to a medical professional (nipples are sensitive and important areas of the body, yikes!). If you do wish to try this yourself do some research first—the Kelly Mom website[k] has a great guide with some important pointers.

If mastitis does develop despite your best attempts to prevent it, it's important to continue breastfeeding. The milk from the affected breast will not harm your baby.[61] At this stage, if you haven't already, you should also consult a physician or lactation consultant.

Treatment options to ask about may include:

---

[k] *Please see https://six-weeks.com/links#14*

- Continuing efforts to clear the blocked duct
- Antibiotics (for bacterial based infections)
- Lecithin (a drug which may reduce the viscosity of milk by increasing polyunsaturated fatty acids[62])
- Varying feeding position to increase drainage
- Pain relief

Getting rest when you have mastitis is vital.[63] Stay in bed if you can, or at least put your feet up whenever you're able!

SOME MOTHERS CAN'T, AND THAT'S O.K.

Often, there can be a lot of pressure on women to breast-feed. The origins of this are understandable—even a small break in breastfeeding can detrimentally affect supply, and in the late nineteenth century, when formula was heavily used in hospitals, many women lost their ability to feed naturally when their babies were taken from them and bottle fed overnight.

A woman's right to breastfeed is now rigorously defended, but unfortunately, this can sometimes result in the pendulum swinging too far the other way, leading to women thinking they *have* to breastfeed, when in fact they don't. Studies show that the psychological pressure to exclusively breastfeed may contribute to postpartum depression in new mothers if they can't achieve their goals.[64] So, it's important to say that some women can't breastfeed. And some women don't want to. The truth of the matter is, there's no shame either way, and certainly no damage to the baby from being formula fed.

In America, though 4 out of 5 women start by breastfeeding their baby, only 57.6% are still doing it at six months, and 35.9% at 12 months of age.[65] We weaned our child at six months. Kate felt like she needed to breastfeed our daughter for as long as possible, and the decision to stop didn't happen until she'd finally had a gutful of the constant blocked ducts and mastitis. But honestly? For the excruciating pain it regularly caused Kate, and the pressure it put on the entire family, we should have stopped much sooner.

It's every family's right to choose how they want to feed their child. Read the chapter titled 'breastfeeding vs. formula' so that your family can make an informed decision after the birth of yours.

FURTHER INFORMATION

The Pressure to Breastfeed (Web Article)
A discussion about the guilt, pressure and depression that can occur when well-meaning clinicians push breastfeeding even when a mother can't or doesn't want to do it.

Please see https://six-weeks.com/links#14 for web links.

15 | BREASTFEEDING VS. FORMULA

I found it interesting that breastfeeding was pushed a huge amount pre-birth, but I was never, ever taught or given any information about formula. Everyone just assumed that I was going to breastfeed, and it felt very much like they were saying 'if you don't, you can figure the rest out on your own.'

Because I did want to breastfeed, I didn't worry too much about the issue. But then my brother died three months after Nathan was born, and just like that my milk was gone. I was so stressed and upset that my body just… shut down.

I needed formula but had no idea what to buy or how much to feed my child. I was terrified I'd somehow hurt my precious baby by feeding him from a bottle! I learned more about formula by perusing the supermarket shelves than in my ante-natal class. That's not how you want to get your information.

So knowing your options is important. Breastfeeding doesn't make you any more real a mother than having legs makes you a good runner. Be educated about your choices before you need to make that decision! Because trust me, it's important. And you shouldn't have to make it standing in a supermarket desperately reading labels.

AMY, MOTHER TO NATHAN

Ooh boy. Buckle up and strap on your helmet because entering the breastfeeding debate is like leaping naked into a war zone. There's a whole lot of propaganda flying left and right, but let's move past all that and cut straight to the facts:

- Breastfeeding is a great way to feed your baby.
- Formula is also a great way to feed your baby.
- Your family's method of feeding will be determined by your situation. The only thing you *need* to do is know both sides of the argument, so you can make an informed decision.

BREASTFEEDING

First up, in a totally enclosed environment *with no external factors*, breastfeeding will always be the best option for feeding your child. It does so much more than just give the energy and nutrients they need to grow. Breastmilk is custom made for each infant, containing a whole heap of things that formula can't—for example, antibodies for the baby and health benefits for the mother. It also saves time and money, and it's portable!

Here's a quick list of some of the more important benefits a breastfed baby receives:

Ideal Nutrition

Powdered formula is a one-size-fits-all experience for a baby. That doesn't mean it's bad—baby formula has been crafted to provide literally every nutrient an infant might need that scientists can think of. But your breastmilk has an exact mix of nutrients that is perfect for *your* particular baby. This mix changes as the baby grows. Additionally, the breasts produce hindmilk at the end of a feed, which has a higher fat content that helps a baby sleep.[1]

---

[1] *To be clear, the milk a breast produces doesn't change during a feed, however the fat content does. Fat in the milk sticks to the walls of alveoli (where the milk is made) but dislodges as the breasts begin*

Antibodies

When the mother is exposed to viruses or bacteria, the antibodies she produces to protect herself are transferred through the milk to help protect the infant. As an infant's immune system is immature at birth, this means breast-milk offers better protection for infants against viruses or bacteria specific to the area where the family lives.[66] Studies have shown that babies who are not breastfed are more vulnerable to health issues like pneumonia, diarrhea and infection.[67]

Reduces Disease Risk

It seems almost magical, but you can't argue with the result of numerous studies. Exclusively breastfeeding your child may reduce middle ear infections by up to 50%, hospitalization from respiratory tract infections by up to 72%, colds by up to 63%, diabetes by between 30-40%, childhood leukemia by 15-20% and a whole host of other issues (including SIDS).[68]

IQ

Studies have shown that breastfeeding—and in particular, exclusive breast feeding (i.e., not giving a child formula at

to empty, thus producing milk with a higher fat content toward the end of a feed.

any stage)—may make a child smarter. To quote a multi-year study that looked at 1300 American breastfed babies:

"We ... assessed several aspects of neurodevelopment at 3 and 7 years, including language, intelligence, visual motor ability, social–emotional development, behavior, and executive function. We found that even after controlling for factors such as socioeconomic status, parental education, maternal IQ, and the home environment, breastfeeding for a longer duration—and especially exclusive breastfeeding for a longer duration—was associated with higher child IQ at school age. Specifically, for each additional month of exclusive breastfeeding, child verbal IQ was 0.8 points higher, translating to a benefit of almost 5 points over 6 months."[69]

Other trials have found similar outcomes, for example one which tested almost 14,000 six-year-olds and found a 7.5-point verbal IQ advantage in those that were breastfed.[70]

For many parents, this is an incredibly strong argument in support of breastfeeding, however it's worth noting a couple of quick caveats:

First, both studies are over 10 years old (and some of the earliest studies are from the 1990s). Some experts believe that the difference in IQ is due to the Omega-3 fatty acids (in particular, DHA) that are found in breastmilk, and subsequent to these studies, many brands of formula have been improved to include this ingredient (look for the 'gold' label on a baby formula tin, which symbolizes that the powder includes additional ingredients over the base mix—almost always, this will include DHA).

Second, mothers with a high IQ are *more likely* to breastfeed, and this can skew results because their children may be naturally smarter, regardless! The most compelling evidence to support this claim comes from a 2006 study of over 5000 siblings, where one child was breastfed and the other wasn't. It found that breast feeding had little or no effect on intelligence in children within the same parental unit.[71]

So, breastfeeding may make your child smarter. *Or it may not*. One thing's for sure though, it certainly won't harm their intelligence.

Reduces SIDS

Breastfeeding for at least two months has been shown to reduce the risk of Sudden Infant Death Syndrome (SIDS) by 50%.[72] There are many theories about the reasons for this. The leading ones include the reduction in respiratory and gastrointestinal infections we talked about earlier, and a reduction in reflux—probably because breastmilk is emptied faster than formula from a baby's stomach.

As well as benefiting the infant, breastfeeding also has proven, evidence-based benefits to the mother:

Helps the Uterus Contract

During pregnancy, a woman's uterus experiences a radical expansion, stretching with the growth of the baby to many times its original size. After birth, it's important for the uterine muscles to contract as this helps slow bleeding. Oxytocin, sometimes called 'the feelgood hormone,' is released during breastfeeding and helps with this process. In the early days, a woman may be able to literally *feel* her uterus clenching when she breastfeeds—it feels like period pain!

Reduced Risk of Breast Cancer

Studies of more than 147,000 women across 30 countries don't lie—breastfeeding significantly reduces the risk of breast cancer. Breastfeeding for any period of time lowers the risk of breast cancer by 14%, breastfeeding for more than a year reduces it by 28%,[73] and every additional year a woman breastfeeds may reduce it even further.[74]

Scientists think the reduction may be linked to the pause that breastfeeding women experience in their menstrual cycles (a woman's period usually doesn't return until after she has stopped breastfeeding). Fewer cycles mean less estrogen in the body, which is known to promote abnormal cell growth. Ergo, less cancer.

Breastfeeding can also help lower ovarian cancer risk for the same reason.

Weight loss

Because of the way the human body stores fat, breastfeeding mothers may initially store more fat than non-breastfeeding mothers, however studies show that this should change around the three-month mark, when breastfeeding mothers experience an increase in their fat burning ability.[75] Of course, the best way to lose weight is still exercise, when the mother feels up to it, but every other little bit helps!

Saves money

According to the US surgeon general, families who breastfeed can save between \$1,200 – \$1,500 per year over those who buy formula.[76] It makes sense when you think about it—breastmilk is free, but baby formula isn't. As a side note, the baby poo of breastfed babies smells much less offensive than when they're formula fed. So… double win!

Convenient

In terms of portability, breastfeeding is super easy—no matter where a mother is, if their child gets hungry they have a built-in, pre-heated, custom made meal they can instantly supply. Just pop the top, latch the lips and the job is done!

FORMULA

As stated earlier, in a totally enclosed environment with no external factors, breastfeeding will always be the best option for feeding your child. But... *no family lives in a bubble*. From lifestyle choices to health issues, and cultural reasons to diet, there are an abundance of reasons why giving your child formula may be the best option.

Modern formula is markedly better than the powdered milk your grandparents or even parents may have used. Formula nutrients and proportions may not be tailored to each individual baby, but they still closely match those found in breastmilk. And sure, breastmilk can help reduce infection... but many babies will not develop severe infections in the first few months, regardless of the method in which they are fed.

Formula is a healthy, safe and excellent way to feed your child should you wish to do so… and, it's worth pointing out, there are millions of healthy, happy, emotionally stable adults walking around today who were formula fed.

Let's look at some more reasons why a family may choose to use formula.

Some Women Can't Breastfeed

Let's start with the most obvious. Some women can't breastfeed—from mastectomies to stress, there are many things that can affect milk production. Medication can also be transferred through breastmilk. Most commonly used drugs are safe for infants that are breastfed, but some medications taken by mothers can be dangerous for the breastfeeding baby. Amiodarone (used to treat heart conditions), lithium (used to treat some mental health disorders), and retinoids (used in the treatment of skin conditions) are all passed on to a baby and can be dangerous.[77]

Bonding

Feeding a child formula means that people other than the birth mother can participate in the activity. Dad or the second mother can help feed a child, as can grandparents and other important caregivers.

Now, it's important to note that formula isn't the only, or even best way of bonding with a child. Partners of women breastfeeding their child can still develop equally strong relationships with their little one. Still, giving a baby a bottle is one very special way that a significant other can help out. Gazing into your child's eyes as they feed is a wonderful experience.

Sleep

In case you hadn't guessed it yet, sleep deprivation in the first six weeks is a killer. Most people can survive one bad night, but no-one gets through a month+ of bad sleep unscathed.

When an infant isn't reliant on breastfeeding, anyone can help out. Partners or grandparents can take evening shifts, and it's possible to employ night nurses and caregivers too. In the first six weeks, the difference this makes shouldn't be underestimated. A good night's sleep (or even just an extra two hours) can help mental health and even save relationships.

It's worth mentioning here that it's possible for breastfeeding mothers to express their milk into a bottle, allowing others to feed their baby, though this still has problems. Even if a woman expresses earlier in the day so she can sleep at night, her breasts don't stop generating milk—they will slowly engorge and wake her even if the baby doesn't need to be fed.

Diet

Sometimes, formula can just fit a heck of a lot better with your lifestyle. Breastfeeding mothers have to watch what they eat and drink, because things like caffeine and alcohol can be passed through breastmilk and into the baby. This may seem small, but looking after your own physical and mental health is an important part of being a parent, and for some people, being able to have a morning coffee or an evening wine can help them feel human.

Babies can benefit too. In most instances a breast will generate the perfect amount of milk for the infant it is feeding, but sometimes it won't. We know of one couple whose breastfed baby cried and cried for weeks and they couldn't work out what was wrong. They ended up giving it a bottle of formula in desperation, and it settled immediately.

It turned out the mother had a low milk supply and the child was just hungry. Nobody knew, because when you're breastfeeding you can only guess how much you're giving your child through things like the number of wet

Tip: Alcohol and Caffeine

Some of the pros and cons of breastfeeding vs. formula aren't black and white, and this is one instance. Breast-feeding women *can* drink wine and caffeine, but they need to be much more careful.

Babies can't get rid of caffeine as easily from their bodies as an adult. It tends to build up over time. One coffee occasionally is generally okay for a breastfeeding woman, however a coffee every day can send your baby into overload!

Alcohol is slightly different. Alcohol levels in breast-milk are the same as alcohol levels in the bloodstream, and are usually highest 30-60 minutes after drinking, but dis-appear about 2-3 hours after. So, the best time to drink that glass of wine is actually when you're breastfeeding! This gives the maximum amount of time for your body to process it before your next feed.

It's important that you only have one drink if you're a breastfeeding mother, as the length of time alcohol stays in breastmilk stacks with each subsequent drink. While one drink can only be detected in breastmilk for 2-3 hours, two drinks hang around for 4-5 hours, three drinks for 6-8, and so on![78] Basically, if you've still got alcohol in your bloodstream, you'll also have it in your breastmilk.

and dirty nappies, whether the baby is still hungry at the end of a feed, and weight gain. With formula, you know exactly how much the baby is getting.

Work

Yes, it's possible to express and feed your baby via a bottle and many working mothers accept this challenge head-on. However pumping at work, or even having your partner bring your child to work so you can breastfeed, simply isn't an option for some people. Working a long distance from home, odd hours, putting your child in day care, a stressful work environment or even an uncomfortable work culture can all be valid reasons to give your baby formula.

Body

Let's talk about *mastitis*. And let's start that conversation by swapping the 'd' in *duct* for an 'f' to describe just how bad it can be.

Mastitis is incredibly painful and can make breastfeeding a horribly uncomfortable ordeal. Just ask any woman who's had it and watch them shudder. Approximately 10% of US breastfeeding mothers get mastitis,[79] and formula feeding your child means you can reduce the risk of this happening.

Additionally, breastfeeding plays around with the hormones in your body. Though it's not 100% effective, breastfeeding can act as a natural contraceptive because it delays the return of ovulation and a woman's period (see the chapter on sex for more information).[80] For those wanting to have more children *fast*, formula feeding can help restore the body to its pre-pregnant equilibrium.

Mind

This one's a catch-all for many of the other points made already, but it's worth stating specifically. The pressure to breastfeed can be intense, and some people are just happier letting all that stress go. Bottle feeding mothers have the potential for more sleep and social freedom, all because other people can help feed the baby. Postpartum depression is a serious issue for new mothers. One in seven mothers will be affected by it,[81] and anything that can be done to lessen this may potentially be in the family's best interests.

WHO RECOMMENDATIONS

The World Health Organisation states that an infant should be breastfed exclusively for the first six months, and then be given nutritious complimentary foods with breastmilk thereafter until the child turns two. It's a strong case to breastfeed, and one that many breastfeeding organizations have used to argue for parents to abandon the bottle.

However, it's worth scrutinizing this argument a little more deeply.

The WHO's recommendations are based on both their own research and importantly, a large, comprehensive review of relevant breastfeeding studies published by the *Cochrane Library*.[82] This Cochrane Systematic Review is 'A Grade' research—the best quality you can get—and its purpose was to support the assertion that exclusive breastfeeding up to the age of six months was safe. It found numerous benefits to exclusive breastfeeding, including reduced gastrointestinal infections in infants, a longer time before the mother's menstrual cycle returned, and it also helped mothers lose weight.

These are all great justifications to exclusively breastfeed! However when the review is read in depth, several further points are made which breastfeeding advocates seem to largely ignore: the review found no difference in infant growth, allergic diseases, obesity, cognitive ability or behavior between exclusively breastfed babies and those who were mix-fed from 3-4 months of age.

Importantly, the Cochrane Systematic Review made zero assertations about the benefits of breastfeeding versus exclusive use of formula—even though the WHO's policy (which references the study as justification) recommends just this!

So why is breastfeeding such a big deal? And why does the WHO push so strongly for exclusive breastfeeding over formula when sure, there are benefits to breastfeeding, but maybe not as many as the average person might think?

Much of the WHO's research focuses on improving outcomes for babies in developing countries. And in many of these countries, issues arise when trying to formula feed that we as citizens in first-world countries aren't exposed to—including access to clean water, the ability to reliably sterilize water before mixing it with formula, and even reliable access to infant formula.

In these countries, a formula fed infant stands a very real chance of catching something from poor quality water, or starving if a family's formula tin runs out and they are unable to get more. Because remember, once a woman stops breastfeeding, it's awfully hard to get that milk supply back.

Realizing this helps put the WHO guidelines in perspective—they're incredibly important, but if you have reliable access to formula, clean water and sterilizing equipment, they may not be the most relevant guidelines for your specific situation. If you want more information about breastfeeding, mixed feeding or formula feeding, talking to your pediatrician will give you the most up-to-date information relative to your circumstances.

YOU DON'T HAVE TO BE EXCLUSIVE

Breastfeeding and formula are a bit like dating. There're a lot of people out there that want you to be exclusive, but in reality as long as all parties are happy, who cares?! Often, there's no harm in double dating. If you take them both out to dinner and introduce them to each other, neither will complain one bit.

Plenty of people, the authors of this book included, breastfeed as much as we can, when convenient and we're able, but top up our feeds with infant formula when we need to—in our case, when Kate had mastitis (which pummeled her milk supply), or travel made breastfeeding challenging, or the baby seemed hungry even after a feed.

So how do you do things intelligently? Well, the biggest risk will be harming your breastmilk supply. If you don't use it, it dries up. As long as you're aware of this, and don't (for example) feed a baby exclusively by formula for multiple days in a row (without expressing) and then try to resume breastfeeding, the occasional bottle won't hurt and may in fact be just what's needed for everyone's sanity. Talk to a medical professional about your situation, what you can safely do without losing the ability to breastfeed, and what's best for your family.

SO, WHAT SHOULD YOU DO?

Ultimately, whether a child is breastfed or formula fed is up to each individual family. What is best for your child depends on your situation.

If you're unsure and looking for direction, our advice is to try breastfeeding first, and if that doesn't work, then consider switching to formula. The reason for this is practical. A woman's breastmilk supply, especially in the early weeks, is incredibly temperamental. Milk supply is based on demand, and if a baby doesn't feed, milk won't be produced.

After the first few weeks, it's also something of a one-way street. It's hard to go back to breastfeeding (but not impossible) if you start with formula first.

When do you know to switch? Well if you ask a lactation consultant they seem to usually say 'just keep trying.' It's well-meaning advice: breastfeeding is hard and takes practice. Many women end up feeding successfully even after initial troubles with the right guidance.

But… sometimes, more objective advice is required. If you want to switch from breastfeeding to formula feeding, talk to your pediatrician or GP. Not only can they guide you through the process, but their outlook tends to be a lot more rounded, focusing not just on what's good for the baby, but also for the mother.

As we said earlier, in a totally enclosed environment with no outside factors, breastmilk has more benefits than any other type of food for your infant. But… no family lives in a bubble. Formula isn't bad for your child. It's still a great way to keep your baby healthy, and in some situations it may even be better! There's no shame in giving your child a bottle if that's what's best for everyone.

The final verdict? At the end of the day *fed is best*. How that's done is up to your family.

FURTHER INFORMATION

The 11 Benefits of Breastfeeding (Web Article)
An excellent, evidence-based article about why breastfeeding is beneficial for mother and child, with links to further reading for each claim the article makes.

Newborns: Bottle Feeding (Web Articles)

A comprehensive 'how to' page with lots of good advice if you decide you want to formula feed your infant, including how to give a baby their bottle, how to sterilize equipment, how to mix formula and a video showing bottle and formula preparation for dads.

The Data all Guilt Ridden Parents Need (Web Article)

A New York Times opinion piece by Emily Oster, author of *Cribsheet*, who examines common parenting myths, including many revolving around the breastfeeding / formula debate, from a data perspective—asking whether the research truly supports conventional claims.

Fed is Best (Website)

The Fed is Best Foundation works to provide families and health professionals with the most up-to-date scientific research, education, and resources to practice safe infant feeding with breast milk, formula, or a combination of both. They also have a Facebook page.

Please see https://six-weeks.com/links#15 for web links.

16 | WONDER WEEKS

*Our daughter is now twelve months old and I'm still not
100% sure what Wonder Weeks are all about. All I know
is that my wife talks about it constantly—it's all the rage
in her mother's group right now.*

MARV, FATHER OF VIOLET

The term Wonder Weeks was first coined in 1992 and
describes 10 periods of intense infant mental development
that happen at predictable times over the first two years.
The first one occurs around week five and is a time when
your baby will be particularly fussy—that's a nice way of
saying you're going to have a very, very hard week because
your baby will cry a lot!

Wonder weeks (also called fussy weeks, or stormy
weeks) are an important concept for new parents because
they can be very tiring, stressful periods. Your infant is

going through monumental changes—in each one, the world suddenly becomes different in some new way—and this can be frightening. Previously happy, content children become grumpy, irritable and clingy. They may want to feed more often, and parents may get less sleep.

On the bright side, this all happens for a reason! In leap one (usually occurring at week five but sometimes appearing as early as week four), an infant undergoes enormous changes to their senses, metabolism and internal organ function. They look at things longer and more often, notice new smells, and are more aware of being touched.

Being bombarded by all these new sensations must be terrifying! Imagine waking up tomorrow with the ability to see and feel twice as much as you could before. What if you could suddenly hear everything in a two-block radius and see behind you as well as in front? Before you thought it was cool, you'd feel overwhelmed. Maybe terrified! It's obviously a silly example, but it helps put into perspective what it must feel like for an infant.

On the upside, it's about this time that your infant may start to smile.

Slightly beyond the six-week scope of this book, but hey—we're feeling generous—leap two occurs sometime between seven and nine weeks of age and is when your

Origins

While the term 'Wonder Weeks' is a relatively new term, the theory behind it has been around since the 1930s. Jean Piaget, a swiss psychologist, disagreed with the then widespread notion that intelligence was a fixed trait and instead illustrated that a child's development is a result of both biological maturation and interaction with the surrounding environment.[83] Or in layman's terms: as children grow, their brains change and become capable of learning and problem-solving challenges in their day-to-day life. It is from this concept that the Wonder Weeks have come into being.

child will start to notice patterns. This is so much more than just black and white squares on a piece of paper. Patterns are an important part of speech development and preclude your child's first attempts at talking with short bursts of *ah*, *uh* and *ehh*.

Leap two is also an important precursor to voluntary movement, such as grasping at toys (when you think of it, a pattern is just something repeatable with the same effect. Knowing that when you reach for it, you'll get a toy is a pattern of thinking all by itself!).

Controversy

The medical community is divided on the legitimacy of Wonder Weeks. With its drawings of cute ducks and fuzzy-wuzzy language, the book is a little 'fluffy' for some professionals.

And though the medical community agrees that there are periods in a child's life where they undergo intense neurocognitive development, many question that there are ten of these distinct periods (a study subsequent to the book's release failed to find them[84] —it only tested four children so isn't very credible, but some professionals still cite it as evidence against the Wonder Weeks' theory).

Our advice to you? *See for yourself.* Preparing for a bad week can't hurt and it might just help (we think it will). If you don't notice any difference around week five, great! If you do, then reading more on this concept may make life a little easier for you all.

Like a reward for getting through a wonder week, the week after is often a wonderful period of calm for both parents and baby. Knowing about wonder weeks (and the week after) is helpful for planning work and visitors. In our household, wonder weeks mean we go into lockdown.

We politely decline visitors, stock the freezer with frozen meals and prepare for a period of no sleep, knowing that there'll be time afterwards for all those things we've missed, once our baby is out the other side.

FURTHER INFORMATION

The Wonder Weeks (Website)
The Wonder Weeks website is a great place to start for free information and the basics of each week. On the website you will also find links to an app and book, should you wish to purchase either.

We found the app handy for its reminders and the quick, easy access it gave to information on our phones. The book tended to have a little more information on each leap as it occurred which we also found useful, so both are good options should you wish to purchase them.

Please see https://six-weeks.com/links#16 for web links.

17 | VISION

I was changing his nappy when I first noticed Gabriel following my hands. Previously, he'd stared at objects statically, but now his eyes tracked my fingers in jerky movements. He turned to me with this big, goofy confused look on his face. "Hey, did you know about these things?" his eyes seemed to say. "They're moving!"

BRIGITTE, MOTHER OF GABRIEL

A child's vision develops rapidly after they are born, but it takes around 4 months to perceive depth,[85] 5-7 months to develop full color vision, and 4-6 years before they have the vision of an adult.[86] At first, an infant will have quite poor eyesight, and will most probably look like they are cross-eyed. This is normal.[87]

In the first few months, your child will be very near-sighted, capable of only focusing around 8-10 inches

(20-25cm) in front of them—just far enough to clearly make out the face of the person holding them.[88] Beyond this distance what they see will be blurry, so get in nice and close when talking to your newborn and giving them cuddles!

In the first few days after birth, an infant will develop a preference for looking at their mother's face over that of a stranger,[89] however they won't be 'seeing' her like an adult. Early infant vision is all about high contrast areas. They won't take in a whole face, for example, but instead see only the boundary between two different areas, such as at a mother's hairline. From very early on, infants can copy some facial expressions and tongue movements.[90] Wriggling your eyebrows and holding your mouth in different positions can be fascinating for your little bundle of joy! It will take a little longer for your baby to be able to respond to different friendly/smiling or non-friendly/expressionless faces.

At first, your baby only sees the world in black, white and shades of grey.[91] Within the first month of life, your baby will start to perceive highly contrasting colors like red, black and white. Or blue, yellow and orange.[92] Other colors will come later. It's fascinating to see a child's eyes lock onto a bright object, and a wonderful sign of their burgeoning capabilities.

At four weeks they may start tracking moving objects very slowly and their tear ducts may also begin to work[93] (sheesh, way to break a parent's heart)! As your baby's parent, your little one will start watching you very closely too![94]

One great activity you can do to engage your child and help their development is print out a series of black and white silhouettes. It doesn't matter what—print something fun for you, as your child won't care if it's a circle or the outline of a Transformer. Initially, hold the picture close and watch as your child studies it. Remember, they're not taking in the whole picture, but rather the line where black and white meet. As they get closer to the six-week mark, place similar images on the wall next to their change table—it can help calm and captivate your baby as their diaper is changed. For our daughter, a Pikachu outline kept her captivated and still when we changed her diaper—prior to this she'd scream every time she was placed on the change table!

Another fun activity is to play shadow puppets. Don't worry if your child doesn't show interest in a silhouette or shadow puppet at first. Remember, they're developing so rapidly that their vision is constantly improving, and therefore the things that interest them are changing too. Try again in another week and see if you notice a difference. It's an amazing experience to see your child stare at something they previously ignored. It's tangible evidence of just how rapidly they develop!

FURTHER INFORMATION

Your infant's vision development: What to know (Website)
This in-depth article, written by a Doctor of Optometry, is almost a fact sheet for the wonderful level of information it contains. If you'd like to know more about your baby's vision, it's a great place to start, discussing everything from focus to premature baby vision to eye alignment problems.

How Much Can Little Ones See? (Video)
This quick, one-minute video replicates what an infant can see at various weeks after birth, moving the camera in and out of focus to give a general timeline. Be warned—it can be a touch confronting to note just how little a child can see in the first few weeks!

Age-Appropriate Vision Milestones (Fact Sheet)

Want specific milestones for what your child will see at birth, 1 month, 2-3 months, 4-5 months and beyond? This page is for you. Though light on details during the first 6 weeks, it may provide a handy reference chart for parents over the first year about when to expect your child to produce tears, look at themselves in the mirror and develop color preferences.

Mesmerised (Book)

A gorgeous black and white book for babies with no words, just high contrast images. We were given one as a gift and our baby fell in love with it from just a couple of weeks of age, staring spellbound at its simple pictures.

Please see https://six-weeks.com/links#17 for web links.

18 | SOUND

I'm so used to having conversations with my infant that I forget how it must look to strangers – this tired woman with bags under her eyes holding a one-way discussion with her six-week-old daughter as she takes her for a walk.

"What are your thoughts on the stock market?"

"Really? Baby industries are bullish?"

"I mean, of course you'd say that—you've got skin in the game."

You can almost see people thinking 'poor woman, she's lost it.'

JACKIE, MOTHER OF ALEXANDRA

Sometimes it seems that the only noise coming from an infant's mouth in the first few weeks is a scream. This may be confronting to some parents who, while not expecting their baby to form words, have had happy daydreams in the months leading up to their child's arrival of interacting with cute gurgles, grunts and coos.

A child can make other sounds immediately after birth (see the chapter on baby language) but the experimental babbles we normally associate with very young babies—those coos and burbles mentioned earlier—will come in the months following birth, not immediately.[95]

You can aid your child's development by showing them 'how it's done.' You don't need to chatter to them nonstop, but talk to your child when you can. Rest assured even if they can't answer back, they'll be listening and learning from the experience.

Researchers think that language is learned in infants through repetition and pattern.[96] When a baby hears the sentences 'here comes the dog' and 'the dog wants a pat' they won't know what either means. But they will (over time) note that there is a similar sound in each, so *dog* must be a separate word. They look for patterns in sentences, and then network those patterns to slowly interpret and learn a language.

So sing and dance and read to your child, from as early as possible. And the noises you make don't have to be specially designed for infants. Play your favorite music! Read the newspaper or the back of the cereal box, or even Lord of the Rings to your child. It's all about expanding their vocabulary and helping them find word patterns.

And when your child does start to babble? Listen, and then smile and talk back, even if it feels like nonsense. This technique teaches them the art of conversation. It encourages them to keep speaking by showing that they're on the right track.[97]

Tip: Language Progression

Technically beyond the scope of this book, but because we know you're interested:

By three months, most babies will be able to coo and gurgle at toys, pets and people. You won't usually get a baby's first words until after six months, and a child will often begin to form short sentences such as 'want milk' between 18-months and 2 years.[98]

Importantly, young children can understand many more words than they can speak. At its simplest, this means you should keep up the conversation from your end and talk to your child about the things they are looking at, and what you are doing. When you're changing their diaper, for example, tell them this. And when it's bath time, talk them through the process.

At the more advanced end of this concept, some parents choose to teach their child sign language to help them communicate, knowing that a child is able to use their hands earlier than they can talk with their mouth.[99] Though it takes dedication and energy that some parents would rather put elsewhere, it can be an amazing experience interacting with your child and having her tell you she's hungry before she can even talk.

If you want to try this, consider starting to teach sign language at around 4-6 months. *The Bump* website has a great list of starter words for American sign language, while *Sign Planet* has an infographic for Auslan (Australian sign language) on their website. You can also see babies of various ages signing on YouTube—it's super cute!

Links to The Bump, Sign Planet and YouTube can be found at https://six-weeks.com/links#18.

19 | SMELL

My baby is like Daredevil in the comic books—he can't see well but he compensates with his other senses. If he had a little red bodysuit, he'd be fighting crime.

JIM, FATHER OF ETHAN

Unlike some other senses, newborns have an amazing sense of smell. It may even be better than our own![100] Their noses develop early within the womb, where they 'breathe in' amniotic fluid, getting used to its taste and smell. After they are born, this familiarity helps them find their mother's nipple, should you choose to breastfeed.

It's amazing to watch—only minutes old, a newborn baby will nose and squirm in the direction of their mother's breast even with eyes fully closed. It seems that breastmilk smells like amniotic fluid, which is why the baby knows where to find it.

As your baby grows, keep in mind this keen sense of smell. You child will use it to identify you[101] long before he can see you clearly, so it's best not to wear overpowering aftershave, deodorant or perfume.

You can also use this knowledge of smell to interact with and stimulate your baby! One fun thing to do after your first few weeks is to create a homemade scent session. Grab a jar of cinnamon or vanilla, then some perfume sprayed on a cloth, a ripe banana and a slice of orange. Waft each one under their nose and watch for a reaction. Your child may like some smells, and frown at others.[102]

You can do the same activity with blossoming flowers. Be careful not to rub the odor on your child's nose, as they have no means of washing it off themselves, and you don't want any scent to be overpowering!

Tip: Familiar Clothing

If you ever have to leave your child with someone they aren't familiar with, give the caregiver a shirt you have worn or a comforter that's been down the mother's top. The familiar smell will help comfort your child while you are away.

FURTHER INFORMATION

The Crawl (YouTube Video)

A baby's sense of smell is amazing! Watch as in this video newborns use it to find their mother's breast for the very first time.

Please see https://six-weeks.com/links#19 for web links.

20 | MOVEMENT

I knew our child wouldn't be able to sit or pick things up. But it was another thing entirely to hold him in my arms and realize he couldn't even support his own head. Once when I was rocking him I looked down to see his head flopping back and forth like a boat on the shoreline.

Yeah, I felt pretty bad about that.

BILL, FATHER OF LUCAS & MACY

This is going to be a reasonably short chapter, because in the first six weeks there's not a lot of physical milestones you're going to notice—though there are several reflexes that a child is born with.

At birth, babies should be able to move their arms and legs, but not control them. They'll be able to root around for a breast (try gently brushing their cheek with your finger, they should turn toward it) and they'll try to suckle on a nipple as well. They'll be able to grip your finger, but it's a primitive reflex and won't yet be intentional.

You may notice they fling their arms and legs out as if they're falling when they're surprised: this is called the startle reflex, or Moro reflex[103] (although similar, technically these two reflexes are different. However as most people use them interchangeably, we'll do the same in this book). It can happen if they hear a loud noise, or you tilt them suddenly backward—for example when putting them down to change a diaper. The reaction is totally normal, and also one of the many reasons why sleeping infants love a swaddle. It holds their arms nice and tight against their body, stopping the reflex from flinging their arms up and waking them from peaceful sleep.

Another interesting thing your child may be able to do from birth is something called the tonic neck reflex.[104] When your baby turns their head to one side, their arm on that side will straighten (for this reason, the move is also known as the fencing posture).

Then there's the stepping reflex.[105] It's something your pediatrician will check for during a routine examination and also something you can try yourself. Hold your baby up so that she appears to be standing on a flat surface even though you're supporting her weight. Your little one will begin to step one foot in front of the other. Be sure to support her head while doing this though!

Some things a baby *won't* be able to do from birth are to hold her own head up, sit, crawl or smile intentionally (though babies do smile by reflex when they get gas!). By the end of your first six weeks, there's a chance your baby will be able to support her own head, and smile, but sitting and crawling will still be several months off.

You can help develop your baby's head control by giving them regular 'tummy time.' This is where you place a child on their stomach, under your close supervision, so that they can strengthen their neck and upper body muscles. Tummy time should start slowly—only a minute or so at first, repeated 2-3 times a day.[106] As the child gets older, they can remain on their stomach for slightly longer periods, but always under supervision.

FURTHER INFORMATION

Newborn Reflexes (Web Article)
You'll find further information on many of the reflexes discussed in this chapter on this great page published by the American Academy of Pediatrics, including when the reflexes appear and disappear.

Tummy Time (Fact Sheet)

All about the basics of tummy time, including age appropriate milestones and tips for 2 weeks, 1 month, 2 months and older. The Pathways website also has many great pages that provide information about child development.

Please see https://six-weeks.com/links#20 for web links.

21 | IMMUNIZATION

Western medicine is well meaning, but it approaches some things with a one-size-fits-all attitude. Given my fertility journey (the doctors said I could never get pregnant, but here I am) I've learned to question everything. I also touch base with my inner knowing.

I don't like the idea of heavy metals in my child's body. I believe in prevention, sure, but don't believe in smashing that crap into such a small human. Especially when, I believe, breastmilk is all the pharmacy he needs to kickstart his immune system.

I'm not ruling out vaccinations in the future (we may need to immunize our child in order to send him to school) but by then I believe his wee body will be stronger, and able to handle the doses. Until then, we'll rely on herd immunity to protect our child.

CINDY, MOTHER OF ALBIE. ANTI-VACCINATION
SUPPORTER

❖

As a junior doctor I worked in an intensive care unit that looked after a 16-year-old boy with measles. His parents had chosen not to vaccinate him.

It was an awful situation. All of the staff were both frustrated and devastated, and watching his parents tear themselves apart with guilt was heartbreaking. They were holding his hand when he died.

I've always looked back at that series of events with regret because I know *that child's death was 100% preventable.*

KATE, MOTHER OF MERRYN. PRO-VACCINATION
SUPPORTER

Infants are born with immature immune systems. Think about it—when they're in the womb, their mother does most of the heavy lifting with regards to protecting them from pathogens that she is exposed to. When they finally arrive in the big, wide world they can't be given the majority of vaccinations straight away—should you choose to do so—until their immune system is a little stronger, which is around six weeks of age (the hepatitis B vaccine is an exception and is routinely given at the time of birth with informed consent).

Before this time, you should try to avoid highly populated places where highly contagious viruses are easily transmissible. Limit visits to shopping centers, amusement parks and conferences with your child, and try to avoid them yourselves if possible so that you don't get sick and pass it on to the baby. And no matter how much a relative wants to visit your tiny new creation, don't let them anywhere near you or your baby if they or their kids are unwell.

THE ARGUMENT FOR AND AGAINST VACCINES

It's almost impossible to escape the debate for or against vaccines. Both sides are absolutely emphatic in their arguments, which can be confusing for new parents—when both sides are saying that the other could permanently harm your child, which path do you choose, and who do you believe?

This book will try to fairly present both sides of the vaccination argument, though this isn't without its own dangers. Globally, 92% of people in the world believe that vaccines are important for children to have.[107] So when we give equal page space to reasons that parents might be vaccine hesitant, please understand that it's in the interests of education, not because the majority of the world believes in it!

So, are the reasons for choosing not to vaccinate valid? Let's have a look at the anti-vaccination argument now.

ARGUMENTS AGAINST VACCINATION

Those against vaccinations, often called anti-vaxxers, are primarily concerned with the effect vaccines may have on themselves or their kids. The concept isn't new—refusing vaccines started back in the early 1800s with the smallpox vaccine, when the idea of injecting someone with part of a cowpox blister generated sanitary, religious, and political objections[108] (in case you're wondering, modern small-pox vaccines are derived from a virus called vaccinia, which is a poxvirus similar to smallpox, but less harmful[109]).

Though religious and philosophical objections still exist to vaccine injection,[110] in this book we'll focus on vaccine safety for infants under the assumption that this is what you'll be most concerned about.

The anti-vaccination movement believes that both the government and medical community exaggerate the safety and benefit profiles of vaccinations whilst down-playing their risks and true effectiveness.[111] The poster child for this movement seems to be a study published in

1998 by Dr. Andrew Wakefield, linking the MMR vaccine with autism.[112]

Though the article at the time was compelling, there were unfortunately several things that were seriously wrong with the paper—information was falsified,[113] and the lead author had a financial interest complimented by many of the arguments he was making.[114]

The article has now been retracted,[115] and Dr. Wakefield has lost his registration with the General Medical Council of the United Kingdom.[116] It should be noted however, that although the medical community almost unanimously rejects his assertions, Mr. Wakefield has never personally retracted his claims. He still lectures on the dangers of vaccination, has produced a film on the issue and is a guest at many events.[117]

A second concern cited by many is that vaccines contain heavy metals. Thimerosal (a form of mercury) and aluminum are both found in vaccinations (one is used as a preservative, the other as a 'booster' to make the vaccination work better). The fear is that these heavy metals have a cumulative adverse effect on children.

Finally, there are a group of anti-vaccination arguments that revolve around first-hand accounts of affected children. Several very real, and tragic, stories can be found online about parents who took their child for a vaccination only to have them pass away soon after from SIDS. While the stories are heartbreaking, it's worth noting that each case only circumstantially points to a vaccination as the reason, and causal links have never been proven. We'll cover each of these issues over the next few sections.

Heavy Metals: Thimerosal & Aluminum

Thimerosal (ethylmercury) was previously used as a preservative in many vaccines but after an initiative to reduce it in childhood vaccines,[118] is no longer used in many countries around the world (America[119] doesn't use it in any childhood vaccine, and Australia[120] and the UK[121] don't use it at all). In most other places, it is now only found in multi-dose vials of the flu shot.

Now, the important thing to know about thimerosal is that this mercury is in a different form to the mercury found in fish that causes mercury poisoning (methylmercury).[122] That tiny difference (in this case, one carbon atom and two hydrogen atoms) means that thimerosal is metabolized differently and more easily than the toxic form of mercury and thus is less likely to build-up in the body.[123]

In the vaccines that do have it, thimerosal is present in such a small dose that the WHO considers them to be safe even when given to both infants and pregnant women.[124] But for those who absolutely don't want to give their child a vaccine containing thimerosal, the good news is that there are forms of the flu vaccine that don't contain this preservative—you just need to ask your primary care physician to order that particular version of the vaccine ahead of time.

Aluminum salts have been used as adjuvants in vaccines for over 70 years.[125] Their use means that the body produces a stronger immune response to the disease being vaccinated against,[126] and that fewer doses of vaccine are needed to give immunity.[127]

Because aluminum is a 'metal' and many metals are harmful to the human body, the presence of it in vaccines causes concern in some people. But the truth is, aluminum is present in all living organisms. We're not quite sure what it does in the human body—there's no scientific evidence that it is used in any biological process—but it is found in most creatures, and indeed also in rocks, soil, water, air, and food. You will always have some exposure to low levels of aluminum from eating food, drinking water, and breathing air.[128]

When you compare the total amount of aluminum that a baby receives in standard vaccinations up to the age of six months (an average of 4.4 milligrams) it's actually less than the amount of aluminum that a breastfed baby will ingest in her diet in that same six-month period (approx. 7 milligrams).[129]

But what happens to the amount of aluminum in a baby's blood after an injection? At a baseline, babies have about 5 nanograms of aluminum in their bloodstream at any time, and this amount doesn't noticeably change after receiving vaccines—even immediately after the injection.[130] To be fair, in high doses aluminum is known to be toxic to nerves within the brain and spine, however these doses far, far, far exceed those in vaccines by an incredible amount. Keep in mind that any substance in high enough doses, even water[131] and oxygen,[132] cause toxicity to the human body, so the fact that aluminum also does this when taken in large quantities is nothing out of the ordinary.

So, there is no evidence to support the removal of aluminum from vaccines for fear of neurotoxicity.[133] Some individual reports in the literature suggest that there *might* be a link between aluminum oxyhydroxide-containing vaccines and chronic fatigue syndrome, however there have yet been no studies that *prove* a relationship between the two.[134] So while it is indeed true that most childhood vaccines do contain aluminum salts, the truly tiny amount per vaccine, the fact that our infants are all exposed to aluminum in their usual diet, and its long history of safety means that vaccination is not something to be avoided purely on a basis of the vaccine containing it.

Vaccines and SIDS

Here's what The World Health Organisation has to say about claims that vaccines are linked to SIDS in an article titled *Six common misconceptions about immunization*:

"One myth that won't seem to go away is that DTP vaccine causes sudden infant death syndrome (SIDS). This belief came about because a moderate proportion of children who die of SIDS have recently been vaccinated with DTP; on the surface, this seems to point toward a causal connection. This logic is faulty however; you might as well say that eating bread causes car crashes, since most drivers who crash their cars could probably be shown to have eaten bread within the past 24 hours.

"If you consider that most SIDS deaths occur during the age range when three shots of DTP are given, you would expect DTP shots to precede a fair number of SIDS deaths simply by chance. In fact, when a number of well-controlled studies were conducted during the 1980s, the investigators found, nearly unanimously, that the number of SIDS deaths temporally associated with DTP vaccination was within the range expected to occur by chance. In other words, the SIDS deaths would have occurred even if no vaccinations had been given." [135]

Herd Immunity

Herd immunity is a term that has gained a lot of media attention lately. It's an argument that many anti-vaccination supporters use as justification for their actions— "I know that if my baby contracts a disease they will die, but I can rely on herd immunity to protect them so I don't have to worry."

Herd immunity in a nutshell is the theory that if everyone else around your child has received all the standard childhood vaccinations, then the odds of your child catching the disease are infinitesimally small because they'll never come into contact with a disease carrier. Pretty simple. If the people around you are immune, the disease can't get through to you.

In a perfect world, this is completely true—your child can be protected without being exposed to the 'risks' of vaccination. The catch is, though, that we don't live in a perfect world. The first thing to be aware of is that herd immunity only works for diseases that are spread by direct person-to-person contact. For a disease like tetanus, contracted from bacteria present in soil, dust and animal waste, herd immunity doesn't work.

The second thing to be aware of is that with an increasing number of parents choosing not to vaccinate their families, the concept of herd immunity starts to fall apart. If you were the only person in your community not to be vaccinated, you might be okay. But unfortunately, it's likely that you're not. With more and more people choosing not to vaccinate, gaps start to appear in that ring of protection, allowing diseases to get through.

Measles, for example, is a highly contagious disease and vaccination rates of 93-95% are required to provide herd immunity.[136] Currently in Australia (where the authors live), vaccination of 1, 2 and 5 year-old children sits at about 91%[137] —not quite enough to rely on herd immunity for protection against measles if your child hasn't been vaccinated.

Not only is herd immunity becoming an ineffective way to protect children from disease, the choice not to vaccinate healthy children reduces herd immunity for people that are unable to be vaccinated. Some people with rare health issues *cannot* tolerate vaccines (people with tuberculosis, for example). For these people, herd immunity is their only defense against getting sick. With the measles vaccination rate already under what is required for herd immunity, choosing not to vaccinate a healthy child only waters down the ring of defense for those that truly rely on it.

ARGUMENTS FOR VACCINATION

Whereas anti-vaccination supporters use individual cases to support their assertions, pro-vaccination supporters rely on research conducted on large groups of people.

Let's start with the basics—immunization has been proven over and over again to actually work. There's a mountain of research we could quote on the issue, but let's instead look at the physical evidence: the Small Pox virus that we mentioned earlier *no longer exists* except in labs, following a global immunization campaign led by the World Health Organisation.[138] Additionally polio, tetanus, influenza, rubella, haemophilus influenzae type B, mumps and diphtheria (among others) are all diseases that were once prevalent, but thanks to immunization are now greatly reduced.[139] And yes, better standards of living and hygiene may have helped reduce these numbers as well (a common anti-vaccination argument). But we just need to look at the recent Corona Virus outbreak to see that a better standard of living isn't enough to stop a virus all by itself.

Moving on from this to the more important issue for worried parents—vaccines are effective, but are they safe for children? Well, this is where we *will* pull in the research—a whole heap of it.

There *are* some risks to taking vaccines. Children will occasionally develop a rash or other mild reaction. Local reactions (e.g., redness) are usually the least severe and most frequent noticeable side effect. Fever may occur less frequently, and severe allergic reactions are possible, but rare.[140] How rare? One child in every one or two million injections may develop a more severe allergic reaction (meaning you're more likely to be struck by lightning than for your child to develop a severe allergic reaction[141]), but even in these cases, the incidence of death is so rare it's almost impossible to calculate.[142]

Moving on to specifically refute the claims of Mr. Wakefield, a 1999 study by researchers at the University College London, UK, found no causal link between vaccination and autism.[143] In 2001 a study by researchers at the California Department of Health Services showed similar findings.[144] And in 2002 a group of researchers studied *every single child* born in Denmark between 1991 and 1998, looking for a link between the MMR vaccine and autism. *That's 537,303 infants.* Again, they saw zero evidence linking the vaccine to increases in autism.[145]

Invasive Investigations

"If your child is unvaccinated and presents with a significant illness, the pediatrician treating them will not be able to rely on herd immunity to ensure your child doesn't have a vaccine preventable disease, as insufficient people are vaccinating to ensure herd immunity.

As a result, they may need to perform more extensive or more invasive investigations and treatments than a vaccinated child.

I have seen this several times, and each time the parent has stated that this wasn't known prior to refusing vaccination, and that after seeing what their child has just gone through, this information may have changed their decision."

Dr. Jamie Ross, FRACP. Pediatrician and father.

Other reports have made similar findings about the safety of vaccines in general, including one which studied 28,000 Canadian children[146] and another which studied 14,000 United Kingdom residents.[147] The American Academy of Pediatrics lists a further 40+ studies on everything from the general safety of vaccines to the effects of Thimerosal, discussed earlier in this chapter.[148]

Scientists and medical professionals take vaccine safety very, very seriously—perhaps because a large, immunized population has so many benefits to humanity, or maybe just because like all of us, they're concerned about their children.

The anti-vax movement bases many of its arguments on a study by one man on 12 children. Compare this to the plethora of scientists and medics who've studied hundreds of thousands of children across multiple continents. It's difficult to draw any other conclusion – vaccines are safe and reliable.

Verdict

To our thinking, much of the vaccination debate misses a very important point. People may argue about side effects, but nobody on either side *is saying that vaccines don't work*. Even if all the anti-vaxxer claims were true (and they're not), would you rather have an immune child with an allergic reaction, or one that dies from a preventable disease?

Vaccines have saved millions of lives around the world, and almost eliminated some of the deadliest diseases ever suffered by humans. If you still have doubts after reading this chapter, talk to your grandparents or elderly members of the community. Ask them what polio was like, and if they'd ever be willing to risk it. Then look at your family history—chances are, even just a few generations ago someone related to you died of a disease which is easily preventable today.

Ultimately, whether you believe vaccines are beneficial or not is your choice. But to us, the decision seems clear.

VACCINES FOR PARENTS AND CAREGIVERS

Should you decide to get yourself and your child immunized (and we strongly, strongly suggest that you do) your GP or pharmacist will know exactly what vaccines you need to get pre- and during-pregnancy, and what vaccines your baby needs to get after being born.

Many parents additionally request that all people who will be around the infant regularly—including grandparents and other relatives—get appropriate shots as well. This should be done several weeks before the baby is born so the vaccines have time to take effect.

There are lots of variables including age and allergies that will determine what vaccines should be requested pre-birth, and it's also important for the mother to have her vaccines at specific times during the pregnancy.

Generally, the following shots are good to ask about before you have your baby:

The Most Important Vaccines

Both of these vaccines help protect against respiratory illnesses, which are easily contracted and incredibly harmful to infants:

- DTaP (diphtheria, tetanus, and whooping cough / pertussis) vaccine[m]
- Flu vaccine

Other Beneficial Vaccines

The theory behind these vaccines is that we want to provide a 'cocoon of protection' around an infant, limiting the likelihood that they will come into contact with something nasty before they are able to deal with it:

- Varicella vaccine
- MMR vaccine
- Hepatitis B vaccine
- Pneumonia vaccine
- Shingles vaccine

---

[m] *Also called 'Tdap' in some countries*

VACCINES FOR THE BABY

The six-week vaccinations will include:

- Hepatitis B
- DTaP (Diphtheria, tetanus, and whooping cough / pertussis)
- Hib (Haemophilus influenzae type b)
- IPV (Polio)
- Pneumococcal
- Rotavirus

It should be noted that the first four vaccines are combined in one single injection. Pneumococcal is a separate injection, and the rotavirus vaccine is given as an oral liquid.

Many infant vaccines are multi-stage immunizations, meaning they'll get additional 'top ups' at a future point. Should you choose to vaccinate your child these 'top ups' will most likely happen at four months, six months and twelve months.

In many states and countries, it is compulsory to vaccinate an infant.

FURTHER INFORMATION

Baby Doctor Mamas (Podcast)

If you're into auditory learning, this podcast is brilliant—and because the women hosting it are neonatologists, i.e., pediatricians that have sub-specialized to only work with neonates (usually defined as babies under 4 weeks of age), they know what they're talking about! Episode 44 discusses the research behind vaccines, and why getting immunized is important.

Do Vaccines Cause Autism? (Web Article)

An educational resource by the College of Physicians of Philadelphia, this surprisingly even-handed article provides a deeper history of the autism / MMR hypothesis, discussing the original scare, the FDA and government response, and then finally the research done afterwards.

Vaccine Myths Debunked (Web Article)

A nice, fast listicle that describes some of the most common misconceptions about vaccines and the evidence that refutes them.

Six Common Misconceptions About Immunization (Series)
Produced by the World Health Organization (and quoted in this chapter), this is a slightly longer but well-written read that gives a much more detailed dive into vaccine myths, why they exist and what the science says.

Choosing not to Vaccinate (Fact Sheet)
A fact sheet released by the CDC that tells parents of un-vaccinated children what to do in the event of an outbreak of vaccine-preventable disease. It also discusses the risks and responsibilities that those parents have for the health and welfare of their child. A great resource for families that aren't traditionally vaccinating.

Appendix 1 has a helpful social media post that some parents have found useful to put up when they get home from hospital. Among other things, it explains the importance of only having healthy visitors to see the baby prior to vaccination.

Please see https://six-weeks.com/links#21 for web links.

22 | SIDS

For some people trauma can wipe your memory, you for-get the details of the horrific event that occurred. That's not the case for me; I remember every detail from the day our son died. At 7.30am I kissed the top of his head, said I love you, and left for work. At 10.11am my phone rang twice and our nightmare began.

I remember the face of the nurse that smiled, the authoritative voice of the lead doctor giving orders, the social workers hovering in the hallway, Reilly's small body stretched out on the table connected to a multitude of machines, the room with the tissues where they deliver the really bad news.

Above all I remember the weight of his body as I car-ried him to bathe him for the last time. I remember how very small and powerless I felt. I remember the primal, heart wrenching sound my husband made when he cried.

I remember that I couldn't sing to our darling boy no matter how hard I tried. I wished with all my heart to comfort him, even though he was already gone.

RAQUEL, MOTHER OF REILLY AND FLYNN

Sudden Infant Death Syndrome, or SIDS, is the sudden death of an infant under one year of age which remains unexplained after a thorough investigation.[149] It's the leading cause of death in children living in the USA aged between 1 month and 1 year.[150]

Which, when you think about it, is just crazy.

In adults, if someone passes away, we usually know why. "He was ninety-four, it was old age," you may say, giving yourself solace. Or, "the cancer took him young, but we did everything we could." It's not often that adults die and we don't eventually figure out the reason. But not-so in infants.

SIDS is a very real and very heartbreaking issue, made more-so by parents having absolutely no idea why it happened. The agony of losing a child is unbearable and is especially cruel when new parents are left wondering what went wrong.

Fortunately, while no-one can ever fully protect their child from this tragedy, there are many things researchers have discovered that *will* lower the risk of it happening.

The American Academy of Pediatrics (AAP), Australia's Red Nose Safe Sleeping Recommendations, SIDS and Kids New Zealand and the UK's Lullaby Trust all overlap in their advice for parents (we'll specifically reference the AAP recommendations here). Feel free to just read the headings if you want the short version, or the descriptions if you want the 'why':[151]

PLACE YOUR BABY TO SLEEP ON THEIR BACK FOR EVERY SLEEP

This is the big one, people. Sleeping your child on their back *dramatically* reduces their risk of SIDS. When this recommendation was implemented in the USA in 1994, SIDS deaths reduced by 53% over the following ten years, coinciding directly with the increasing practice of sleeping infants on their backs.[152]

This may be because tummy sleeping increases the risk of a baby re-breathing their own exhaled breath, leading to carbon dioxide build up, and also creates the potential for upper airway obstruction and overheating. If there's one thing you can easily do to protect your child, this is it—and this is an important thing to remember when talking to older caregivers, as the recommendation is relatively new.

It should be noted that laying your child on their back won't increase their risk of choking—infants regurgitate a lot, but are also remarkably good at swallowing these posits, or tilting their heads to the side.

USE A FIRM SLEEP SURFACE

Mattresses made for adults are generally too soft and not suitable for infants, who should be placed on a firm sleep surface (e.g., a mattress in a safety-approved crib) covered by a fitted sheet with no other bedding or soft objects to reduce the risk of SIDS and suffocation.

A firm surface maintains its shape and will not indent or conform to the shape of the infant's head when the infant is placed on the surface. Soft mattresses, including those made from memory foam, could create an indentation that increases the chance of rebreathing or suffocation if the infant is placed on, or rolls onto, their stomach.

BREASTFEED YOUR CHILD

Breastfeeding is associated with a reduced risk of SIDS. The protective effect of breastfeeding increases with exclusivity, however, any breastfeeding has been shown to be more protective against SIDS than no breastfeeding.

This may be because breastfed babies are more easily aroused from sleep than formula-fed babies at 2–3 months of age (meaning they can wake if something is wrong), which is around the peak of when SIDS occurs.[153]

HAVE YOUR INFANT SLEEP IN YOUR ROOM, CLOSE TO BUT NOT IN YOUR BED FOR AT LEAST THE FIRST 6 MONTHS.

There's a little argument around the timeframes for this one—most experts agree that a baby should sleep in the same room as their parents for the first four months. After this, opinion is divided.

The AAP recommend a baby sleep near their parents for six months at a minimum but ideally the first year of an infant's life. However Emily Oster, author of *Crib-sheet*,[n] believes this recommendation is short-sighted.

"The vast majority—up to 90 percent—of SIDS deaths occur in the first four months of life, so sleeping choices after four months are very unlikely to matter for SIDS. This also shows up in the data. The choice of sharing a room, or even sharing a bed, does not seem to affect SIDS risk after three or four months, at least for parents who are nonsmokers. This means there is seemingly no

---

[n] *Please see https://six-weeks.com/links#22.*

benefit to extending room sharing for so long. There is however, a real cost: child sleep." [154]

She goes on to argue that sleep studies have shown that if children are put in their own room by four months of age, they will sleep the same amount of time but for longer stretches. This is also the case for children at nine months of age, and the effect is still present much later—children who slept alone by the age of nine months slept for forty-five minutes more each night at the age of two and a half years old than those who didn't.

Sleep is incredibly important for a child's brain development. Not to mention a parent's sanity! In the end, what you do here is up to you—but just remember: everyone agrees the first four months in a parent's room are important. After that, it comes down to how concerned you are about SIDS vs. your child getting a good night's sleep, and your own mental health.

KEEP TOYS AND LOOSE BEDDING OUT OF THE CHILD'S SLEEPING AREA AND KEEP THE HEAD AND FACE UNCOVERED

Older readers will remember a time when a child's cot was crowded with stuffed toys and blankets. It's easy to understand why—tiny babies look very lonely in a huge crib, and familiar objects can seem comforting.

Unfortunately, many of these objects create a very real suffocation risk, which is why the AAP now recommend that a cot be kept clear of all non-essentials. This means your bassinet should have a baby and pretty much nothing else. No pillows, comforters, sheepskins or stuffed animals. Even blankets should preferably be swapped for infant sleep clothing, such as wraps and baby swaddles, and these should not include a hood of any kind.

GIVE YOUR CHILD A PACIFIER WHEN THEY SLEEP

Researchers aren't quite sure why, but studies have shown pacifiers can help reduce the incidence of SIDS, and this is true even if it falls out of the infant's mouth. It doesn't need to be re-inserted after a child falls asleep, and it's important not to hang it around the infant via string or attach it to the child's clothing (as this introduces the risk of strangulation).

For breastfed infants, pacifier introduction should be delayed until breastfeeding is firmly established. Infants who are not being directly breastfed can begin pacifier use as soon as desired.

AVOID SMOKING

By now, most people know the risks of smoking while pregnant, which include pre-term birth, congenital defects and harm to a baby's brain and lungs.[155] Smoking while pregnant also increases the risk of SIDS astronomically (one analysis of over 60 studies concluded that one-third of SIDS deaths might have been prevented if all fetuses had not been exposed to maternal smoking in utero).[156]

However, smoking after your baby is born is also dangerous. Seriously, you can debate all you want about putting your child in their own room after four months, but *do not smoke around your baby.* There is a strong link between smoking and SIDS even when parents smoke away from their babies. The smoke on your clothes can be harmful! Infants have small airways and their bodies are still developing. Smokers should be particularly careful of bedsharing with their infant (even if they don't smoke in bed) as the risk of SIDS becomes particularly high.

AVOID ALCOHOL AND ILLICIT DRUG USE

The experts all agree that drugs are bad, but the 'alcohol' part of this heading is a little more contentious. Once the baby is born, many doctors and midwives unofficially see no problem with a parent or carer having a single drink to unwind every now and again—parenting can be stressful! Current SIDS guidelines, however, state that alcohol should be avoided completely.

The dangers from both alcohol and illegal drugs seem to revolve around two key areas—breastfeeding (because substances may be passed onto the baby) and co-sleeping (presumably, because of the effect substances may have on the parent such as making them unable to respond appropriately to their baby's needs, though the guidelines don't explicitly say).

Illegal drugs are a definite no. If you drink alcohol, do so in moderation (see our 'how to' tip in the *Breastfeeding vs. Formula* chapter). And again, SIDS guidelines officially state you shouldn't drink anything at all.

AVOID OVERHEATING

Several studies have shown that overheating infants can contribute to a higher risk of SIDS. No organization that publishes sleep guidelines advise a specific room temperature, however all advise common sense. "Infants should be dressed appropriately for the environment, with no greater than 1 layer more than an adult would wear to be comfortable in that environment."[157] They also advise that caregivers avoid dressing infants in head coverings (such as hats and beanies) when an infant is sleeping. This is because infants predominantly regulate their temperature through their head and face.[158]

IMMUNIZE YOUR CHILD

Studies have proven over and over again that vaccines are safe to give to infants, and that they effectively prevent the development of a variety of diseases.° Infants are at increased risk of SIDS if they have not received their six week, three month and five month immunizations.[159]

PRACTICE TUMMY TIME

One of the good things that parents have lost with the recommendation that infants now sleep on their backs is the strengthening of the neck and shoulders that stomach sleeping previously produced (when an infant awoke, it would try to lift its head, which gradually exercised these muscles and made them stronger).

° *If you'd like to examine the research yourself, the American Academy of Pediatrics has a summary of many of these studies, categorized by potential parent concern. We've put a link on our website, which you can find at https://six-weeks.com/links#22.*

It is now recommended that infants spend supervised 'tummy time' while they are awake to help combat this (and prevent flattening of the back of the head). Among other things, strong neck muscles help an infant move their head when required to avoid the risk of suffocation.

MORE

The preceding information is an amended list, showing some of the more important SIDS recommendations. For those that enjoy a little 'light' reading, a full list, including links to the data behind these recommendations, can be found online in the AAP's excellent but lengthy article titled *SIDS and Other Sleep-Related Infant Deaths: Updated 2016 Recommendations for a Safe Infant Sleeping Environment*.[160] For Australian audiences, further information can be found on both the Red Nose website and the Raising Children Network website. For UK audiences, additional information can be found on the Lullaby Trust website. New Zealand audiences can find additional information on the SIDS and Kids website, and Canadian audiences can find information on their Government's website.[p]

---

[p] *Please go to https://six-weeks.com/links#22 for all links.*

Many other countries have their own SIDS related information. We encourage you to look up your country's guidelines.

Tip: SUID and SUDI

You will often hear the term SUID (Sudden Unexpected Infant Death) or SUDI (Sudden Unexpected Death in Infancy) used in conjunction with SIDS. Think of them as umbrella terms—SUID/SUDI include all sudden deaths by a baby under one year, including those which we can eventually explain (for example, if a baby dies of a known disease or asphyxiation). SIDS is a subgroup of this, counting only those deaths where we have no idea why they happened. It is a diagnosis of *exclusion*—all other known/possible causes have been ruled out, and the cause of death is still not identified.

For all intents and purposes, you don't need to worry too much about the terms except to know that they exist.[q]

---

[q] *Of note to those who wish to look deeper: Because SUID / SUDI & SIDS mean slightly different things, which term you use when searching for data can give slightly different* (cont. over page)

CHARITIES

There are some great charities out there if you'd like to support research or families affected by SIDS:

The Smiley Reilly Project
Full disclosure, the authors know the founders of this charity personally—Raquel & Jonathan lost their beautiful boy Reilly to SIDS when he was six months of age (Raquel kindly gave the quote at the start of this chapter). The charity provides fun, positive experiences to help families stay together and support each other following the death of a child.

(cont.) *results. For example, SIDS is the leading cause of death in children aged between 1 month and 1 year of age but is 'only' the fourth highest cause of death in infants, including the first month.*

The leading cause of infant deaths in the USA in 2013 was congenital malformations, which accounted for 20.3% of all infant deaths. The second leading cause were disorders related to short gestation and low birth weight (17.9% of deaths). The third leading cause was newborns affected by maternal complications of pregnancy (6.8% of deaths). All of these fall under the classification SUDI, but not SIDS (which is unexplained) and happen predominantly in the first month. SIDS was the fourth highest cause.

American SIDS Institute

This organization takes donations for research, for those who want to donate to find a cause.

Red Nose Australia

The Red Nose organization has a mission to reduce the number of child deaths through miscarriage, stillbirth and SIDS to zero through research, advocacy and education.

FURTHER INFORMATION

SIDS & SUID Data and Statistics (Fact Sheet)

Compiled by the CDC, this page gives SUID (including SIDS) statistics with an American focus, including prevalence by ethnicity and State.

Substance Use During Pregnancy (Fact Sheet)

Produced by the CDC, this quick examination of opioid, marijuana, tobacco and alcohol use while pregnant explains why each is dangerous and provides links to more information (and helplines).

Educational Brochures and Posters (downloadable)

Red Nose Australia's collection of easy-to-read educational brochures and posters addressing safe sleeping, wrapping, tummy time and cot-to-bed transition.

Cribsheet (Book)

If you'd like more information on Emily Oster's argument that infants need to only sleep in their parent's room until four months of age (as opposed to the AAP's 12-month guidelines), this is the book to get. Despite relying heavily on facts and research data for answers, it's a very easy read.

The full list of AAP recommendations for SIDS prevention (Research Article)

Written by the American Academy of Pediatrics, this is the 'bible' of SIDS guidelines that almost every other website, book and article you will read base their information on. Neatly ordered, the guidelines are most useful if you enjoy delving into the *why* behind the recommendations.

❖

Common SIDS and SUID Terms and Definitions
(Fact Sheet)

A quick list and explanation of some of the terms often used when talking about SUID.

Evidence Base for 2016 Updated Recommendations
(Technical Report)

If your concept of 'a little light reading' is sitting down with an encyclopedia, this 36-page report may be just your cup of tea. As the title says, it provides an evidence base for the 2016 SIDS recommendations. Don't read while driving or operating heavy machinery…

Reduce the Risk of SIDS & Suffocation (Fact Sheet)
An easy-to-read summary of the SIDS guidelines on the American Academy of Pediatrics website, with an optional audio download to more information at the bottom of the page.

Please see https://six-weeks.com/links#22 for links to all charities and resources.

23 | PROFESSIONAL PHOTOGRAPHY

We got baby photos done when our little one was just a few weeks old. They're beautiful, but then of course we'd think that—it's our kid! Baby photos are one of those few things that a professional photographer can't really do wrong. They could be the worst photos in the world, but they're of your baby, so you'll be proud as punch. As long as there's one that features your bubbly-wup sleeping in a basket or on a giant flower, they're pretty much safe.

RENEE, MOTHER OF SALVATORE

"What?" We hear you say. "A chapter on professional photography—but isn't this book about babies?"

Well… yes. This will be a short chapter, but at the start of this book we promised a tome filled with the important information other books leave out, and this is one such case.

The first few weeks of your new baby's life are a golden opportunity to get some cracking photos, should you so desire. It can be a relatively cheap thing to do and creates a lasting memory forever (not to mention a great cover for those birth announcement cards your mother-in-law is saying she doesn't care about, but totally wants to see).

The trick to this though, is that new parents are often so busy that they don't get around to organizing baby photos until it's too late. The best time to take newborn photos is when your new baby is between 4-10 days old. During this time, infants sleep a lot—it may only be in short bursts, but professional photographers can work with this 'quiet sleepiness' to produce some amazing shots! Plus, to be honest, babies at this age just look so darn cute—even if you're too sleep deprived to notice! We have incredibly fond memories of our baby shoot—mostly because, as exhausted parents, we got to sit back and watch someone else take care of our child for three hours. We even learned a few tricks; like when the photographer gently rubbed his thumb from the center of our baby's forehead down between the eyebrows, encouraging our child to close her eyes and go to sleep!

Professional photography is one of those things you can organize before the baby comes along too. It takes time to trawl through websites, ask for recommendations from friends and decide on a photographer. Once you've got one, you can enquire about prices and then wait for the baby to be born before deciding on a date (most photographers are flexible—they know babies don't always arrive when they should!).

If you decide you'd like to try a little photoshoot yourself, rather than paying a photographer, you can also plan ahead. The weeks leading up to the birth are a great opportunity to look at professional websites for inspiration, bookmark ideas and make or order props online. There's a lot of great blogs out there with tips, but here's some general advice to get you started:

- Keep the baby warm.
- Feed the baby, then wait till she's sleepy before starting.
- Use natural lighting if possible.
- Keep the background simple.
- Plan your poses. It's okay to take time to settle the bub slowly into them.
- A bean bag, blanket or basket filled with bright towels make great simple props. But be sure never to leave your child unattended!

- Sink to your baby's level—get on your stomach for some of the shots from a different angle!
- Be wary of flash photography as this can be dangerous and hurt a baby's eyes.

Time lapse photography can also be a fun way to record your baby's development—if you have the patience for it. The concept involves taking weekly or monthly photos or videos and then stitching them all together to show your child growing over time.

If you plan to give this a try, keep the camera a set distance from the child each photo (so that the baby grows larger within the frame over time) and it can also help to have a constant background and favorite teddy or other toy as well (again, so that you can see your child growing larger in comparison). Watching your loved one sit in an armchair with a huge teddy beside them and grow slowly larger than the bear is fantastic fun!

FURTHER INFORMATION

Newborn Photography Tips (Web Article)
There's a lot of newborn photography articles around on the internet, but we like this one for its cute inspirational photos which are great if you're trying your own hand at the art. They just make us go *aww…*

One Second Every Day (App)
The difficult thing about doing a time lapse series is actually stitching the content together at the end. This app solves that problem, though there are plenty of alternative programs out there too. If the one-second-per-photo/video limit on the free version (or slightly longer limit on the paid version) doesn't suit, make sure you look around!

Please see https://six-weeks.com/links#23 for web links.

24 | GRANDPARENTS

When I was young my parents would send me into the store to buy cigarettes while they waited in the car. If I was lucky, on the ride home they'd let me light one for them.

Times have changed since then, and so have my parents. But is it any wonder when I had children of my own that I sat the new grandparents down and went through a few do's and don'ts?

RACHEL, MOTHER OF BOBBIE AND KATIE

Research into many aspects of a child's life and well-being has advanced considerably in the past few years. This is great for you as a new parent, but can sometimes lead to difficulty with older relations who may be out of date with modern recommendations. There are many things that were common even just a couple of decades ago which are considered unsafe or inappropriate now. These include:

- Putting babies to sleep on their stomachs
- Spanking
- Not following car seat rules
- Introducing solids before four months of age, including applesauce and rice cereal
- Rubbing whiskey on an infant's gums
- Giving a breastfed infant water before six months
- Putting pillows or stuffed animals in a crib
- Reinforcing gender or race stereotypes
- Using baby powder (considered essential back then, but at best is not required now, and can be dangerous if it's talc)
- Putting methylated spirits on the belly button cord to dry it out
- Leaving the baby alone in the car while popping into the shops or paying for petrol
- Allowing a child to 'cry it out' without approval
- Putting honey on a pacifier to help the baby take to it (wild honey may contain clostridium botulinum spores which, when ingested by infants under the age of 1 year, causes infant botulism)[161]

Consider having a discussion with the central people in your life to check their viewpoint on these and other important issues. But don't make it an interrogation! Just mention some of the things you 'recently discovered yourself,' and ask them their opinion. Most older people will react positively to new information if they're not made to feel stupid. Start by talking about the things you didn't know yourself, then move into a two-way conversation.

It will be important when you have your baby that you educate your parents on how you want your child to be raised. They may even appreciate it! Don't forget that if this is the first grandchild, it may have been years and years since the new grandparents had to calm a screaming infant or change a diaper.

If there are things the grandparents don't know, or they'd like to brush up on their knowledge, perhaps (if we can be excused for a little blatant self-promotion here), you could even consider buying them this book!

FURTHER INFORMATION

12 New Things Grandparents Need to Know (Web Article)
A fun, light blog with some salient points about things that new grandparents should know.

See https://six-weeks.com/links#24 for a link.

25 | SEX

After the birth of our son my wife explained it thus—like a car, she was up on blocks at the mechanics for a while. But if I was patient, revved her the right way and made sure the bills were paid, there'd be one day soon when I could take her for a drive again.

JAMES, FATHER OF CELESTE & CONNOR

Sorry guys and gals, but in the first few weeks, the chances are that sexy time just ain't going to happen.

A woman's body needs to heal—no matter if the birth is vaginal or cesarean, there's a whole lot of stretching and tearing that has just gone on. Even afterward, you'll be so dog-tired that honestly when you can spare twenty minutes,[r] you'll prefer to be sleeping.

---

[r] *Optimism is a virtue!*

Tip: Contraception

Breastfeeding is often touted as a natural contraceptive, and to some extent this is true. If a series of conditions are met (including that the baby is less than six months old, the mother has not had a period since the baby was born and the mother is breastfeeding exclusively) breastfeeding is 98% effective in preventing pregnancy.[162]

It is incredibly important to note the conditions attached to this. Breastfeeding as a natural contraceptive *must* be done properly to have a chance at working. It's not enough just to breastfeed. You need to breastfeed exclusively. *And* your infant must be under six months. *And* the mother's period mustn't have returned. And even then, effectiveness is not 100%. People *can* and *have* fallen pregnant while breastfeeding.

If a breastfeeding mother decides that she wants to go on the Pill as an additional precaution, she should enquire about the 'mini pill,' which is a contraceptive that doesn't contain estrogen, a hormone which can interfere with milk production.

There is light at the end of the tunnel though. One Australian study of 1500 women showed that by six weeks, 53% of women had attempted some form of sexual activity, with just over 40% trying intercourse. This increased to 78% by twelve weeks and 94% by six months.[163]

FYI, the same study showed that women who'd had any form of complication with their birth, be it an episiotomy, perineal tear, assisted vaginal birth or cesarean, were more likely to avoid attempting sex at all within the first six weeks.

So… don't despair. And this goes out especially to the partners. This is an intense period in your lives that you *will* get through. You're not alone—the majority of other parents aren't having sex in the first six weeks either (no matter what your friends are saying). But it will happen when you're both well rested and ready.

The important thing is that you talk about any feelings that you have with your partner. Two people at the same level of sexual desire is not a problem, be that anywhere on a scale from cold to hot. But different temperatures can lead to complications if there's no understanding.

And remember, sex isn't the only way a couple can show intimacy. Quick cuddles, a peck on the lips or even just sitting down together for five minutes with a cup of coffee can do wonders for a relationship.

FURTHER INFORMATION

Sex and Intimacy after a Baby (Fact Sheet)
A great, no-nonsense article on the *Raising Children* website answering many of the questions new parents will have about sex, including timeframes, contraception and physical changes. The video on this page of parents discussing the impact of children on their sex life is also well worth watching.

Sex after pregnancy: Set your own timeline (Fact Sheet)
Another great fact sheet, this time by the *Mayo Clinic.* References at the bottom of the page provide even further information for those who would like it.

Breastfeeding, Fertility, and Family Planning (Website)
A closer look at the the Lactational Amenorrhea Method (LAM), aka 'Breastfeeding as a Contraceptive.'

Please see https://six-weeks.com/links#25 for web links.

26 | BUYING A PRAM / STROLLER

The first time we tried to buy a stroller was at a baby convention. It was an absolute nightmare. We'd thought the fair would be a great place to research baby products, but all the assistants cared about were sales. Customers were lined up literally 10 people deep around them, thrusting cash and credit cards in their direction. They had no time to answer our questions.

'I've missed something,' I remember thinking. 'How do these people even know what they're looking for? Somewhere, at some time, there was a class and everyone went but me.'

We ended up walking away without talking to anyone. A month later, during a period when we knew our local baby store would be quiet, we walked in and asked for advice. We were honest, telling the salesperson that we weren't going to buy a stroller that day—we just needed to know what the hell we were doing.

He laughed. 'You and every other parent!' he said. 'Most of my business is from people I talk to, who come back later.'

His advice was not to worry too much about what you think the baby will need in a stroller—you have no idea what they will be like, and all strollers come equipped with the basic essentials. Rather, new parents should look more at practicalities—will the stroller be comfortable for you? Will it fit in your car? It was great advice. We spoke to that salesperson for over an hour. A week later, we came back with our credit card.

JODIE, MOTHER OF ETHEL

The terms 'pram' and 'stroller' are often used interchangeably, however on a technical level a pram is used to carry very young babies, while a stroller is used after a baby is able to sit up and support the weight of their head. In the US, strollers are also often called a *buggy* or *pushchair*. To avoid confusion, we'll use the term *stroller* to encompass everything, unless specifically stated otherwise.

Shopping for strollers can be confronting—large baby stores often stock what seems like hundreds of models, with top-tier versions costing thousands of dollars. Let's try and break down what you need here, so you don't go cross-eyed later:

SEPARATES VS. CONVERTIBLES

First up, you'll need to decide if you want to buy a separate pram and stroller, or something convertible that can change from one to the other (hint: convertible is the way to go!).

There are two basic types of convertible stroller. One which comes with a bassinet attachment that can then be swapped out for a seat as your baby grows, and the other that just has the one seat that reclines at different angles. It lays flat to safely carry your newborn, then adjusts toward vertical over time. Strollers that are unsuitable for newborns will not lie flat; generally these are suitable from 6 months.[164] It doesn't really matter which one you choose, the main difference (apart from aesthetic look) is that bassinet strollers are generally a bit more expensive (because you have to buy the bassinet and then a separate seat), but the bassinet can often be removed and used to carry the baby inside without disturbing them, while an 'all-in-one' stroller can't.

PRICE TIERS

Strollers seem to come in three price tiers—at least in our opinion. These usually relate to the quality of the device, as well as how many features and extras they have.

At the lower end, a basic model will get your child from point A to point B with a minimum of fuss but may be either heavy and unwieldly, or light and flimsy (it's possible to buy 'umbrella strollers' from many department stores which fold up almost as small as an umbrella. These are great for when you go on vacation, but aren't suitable for infants and don't have great head support for toddlers).

At the upper end of purchasing options, you'll find excellent quality strollers which are often very lightweight with strong frames and a whole lot of gadgets and attachments. These are the strollers to go for if you want to buy a car seat capsule that removes from the car and clips into a stroller (so you don't have to wake the baby if they fall asleep—very useful!). These are also the strollers to purchase if you simply *must* have an insulated cup holder for your low-Cal non-dairy orange mocha-frappuccino (don't laugh, we did!).

Strollers in the middle are often a good option for the budget conscious. Perhaps not quite so feature dense as the top tier strollers, these models still have lightweight, strong options that not only get you and your bub from A to B, but also make the journey pleasant.

WHAT TO LOOK FOR:

In our opinion the three most important features of a stroller, in order, are:

Safety

They don't have to be armored tanks, but strollers should meet the safety requirements of your country (something to remember if purchasing online).

At a minimum, check for a strong brake, sturdy frame, sun protection and a harness (while any harness is better than none, a five-point harness is best. This straps like a rally car seatbelt over both shoulders, around the waist and between the legs). Another useful feature to keep your eyes peeled for is a wrist strap for the stroller operator—it loops around the wrist so that you're still tethered to the stroller on the off-chance that your hand slips and you accidentally let go—though these can be purchased separately as well.

Check to make sure that your stroller is rated as newborn suitable, meaning it can be used from birth if you wish to take your precious little bundle out from an early age. And double-check whether your stroller includes a footrest for your child when they turn into a toddler—that way their feet don't hit the ground.

Portability

If you have a car, chances are you'll be folding and lifting your stroller in and out of the trunk a lot, and the lighter it is, the easier life will be on your back and arms. Before purchasing, try folding it down to ensure the mechanism is easy to operate, and the stroller can be picked up comfortably. Then, check the collapsed size against your car trunk to make sure it fits!

Wheel Quality

This is perhaps a contentious addition to the 'essential' list, but as parents ourselves we think good wheels are a must. You'll be using a stroller to push an increasingly heavy child for the next several years. Wheels that roll smoothly will make the experience just so much more pleasant.

Look for swiveling front wheels as they'll be easy to maneuver, and as a general rule the larger the wheel the better—they'll make the stroller easier to roll.

Don't worry too much about suspension in a stroller unless you buy a jogger—babies often like a bumpy ride, particularly when you're trying to get them to sleep. That said however, inflatable or rubber filled wheels will let you go off the beaten path without shaking your baby to bits. And you probably *will* go off the beaten path, even if it's only walking adjacent to the pavement but not on it. Many parents find this an effective way to add slow, gentle bumps to the pram ride that help lull their child to sleep.

Many baby stores that sell strollers have flour bags of differing weights that you can push around in the models that you're considering buying—don't be scared to see how a stroller will feel when your baby is on board.

ADDITIONAL FEATURES:

After safety, portability and wheels, there are many additional features which may be important depending on your situation:

Convertible to Two-seater

If you're planning on having more than one child, buying something that can accommodate two children now may save you time and money later. Side-to-side two seaters give the best visibility for your children but look strange when you only have that first child.

Other, more expensive strollers get around this by having a separate attachment that usually goes underneath the first child's seat. Baby one sits slightly higher, while baby two sits lower to the ground. The strollers look a little like bobsleds, if that helps get the idea across.

If you're unsure what you want to do, just buy what suits you best now and worry about that second child later, upgrading your stroller if required—some parents with two children simply buy a step or seat that clips to the back of a single seater stroller with its own set of wheels, so their older child rides shotgun as if on a trailer.

Reversible

You'll want to keep a close eye on your newborn when using a stroller, and they'll want to know that you're close as well. Having the option to flip your child's seat around so that they can face you will make both things easier. In the first few weeks, it means you can talk to your child, watch out for vomit and be in their eyeline—even if what they see is a little fuzzy.

As they grow older, it may also aid their development. Adults are much more likely to talk to their children if they are facing toward them rather than having the child face out,[165] and this chatter can both help their linguistic skills and reduce anxiety.[166]

Not that parents need to talk to their child constantly during a walk! Sometimes just getting out of the house is struggle enough. But rearward facing seats and carriers can make conversation easier when it happens.

Dr. Suzanne Zeedyk, a senior lecturer in developmental psychology at the University of Dundee in Scotland, explains why this is important:[167]

"Babies don't need constant attention... they need *enough* attention. And they need it at crucial times. Babies especially need attention and comforting when they are feeling uncomfortable and at risk of being overwhelmed... Having a buggy that faces away, especially probably during the first year, makes it more difficult to let your mum or dad know that you are needing them. The more time that babies have to spend in anxiety, the more their brain comes to expect anxiety, and thus goes on to actually create it."

Jogging Options

Jogging strollers generally have three pneumatic wheels and are specifically designed for running—usually with plenty of room between the handle and wheels so they don't clip your legs, and suspension for the baby so they don't fly from the pram at every bump.

Jogging strollers are not recommended for newborns and infants. Despite having excellent head and neck support (usually the strollers allow infant car seat carriers to be attached to a stroller frame), babies can still suffer injury.

The problem, as one pediatrician explained to us, is that even with the best padding and suspension, at running speed the tiny oscillations in the carrier and frame of a jogger become violent enough to potentially cause micro hemorrhages in an infant, causing bleeding from the tiny, fragile little vessels in the back of the eye.

That said, when it *is* time to use a jogger safely (most pediatricians recommend six months of age, with full head control) look for strollers with excellent suspension, and only plan to run on smooth surfaces until your bub is much older.

Remember: young infants are *very* fragile. Hard shaking or jolting can do serious and permanent damage, so it's important you take every possible step to prevent this from happening.

Height

Are you or the people most likely to push your baby in his stroller very tall or short? If so, it's well worth getting out there and testing any potential strollers in person. Check how easily you can retrieve a child from their seat or bassinet, and how the stroller feels when you are pushing it. Many strollers have adjustable handles, which are worth looking into, and check the position of the rear axle—this may cause issues for people with long strides if they clip them as they walk.

Storage

Yes, the primary purpose of a stroller is to push your child. But you're also going to have to carry a nappy bag, your own purse or wallet, and like it or not bags of groceries at some stage too. It's helpful to have a compartment (usually underneath the child's seat) to store items – otherwise, you'll be the one lugging them in one hand while you push the stroller in the other. Some strollers come with bag hooks that attach to the handle. Alternatively, you can purchase bag hooks separately and attach them to your stroller handle yourself (it's easy). These hooks can be useful for smaller bags that aren't too heavy, or so long that they get tangled in the wheels or bump your legs when you walk.

Travel Systems

Some strollers are designed to not only take interchangeable bassinets and seats, but also special car seat capsules which can be removed from the car and clipped into the stroller frame. Buying a car seat and stroller that work together means you'll have a better chance of keeping your baby asleep after the car ride when you reach your destination. It will also mean less hassle when you make a quick trip to the shops or visit friends—just unclip the capsule from the car, snap it into the stroller, do your thing and then put bub back in the car, all without waking him.

Peripherals

Many strollers have a whole host of optional extras you may (or may not) want to consider after purchasing the main frame—everything from coffee cup holders to rain covers, should you be caught in bad weather. The more expensive the stroller, the more peripherals it may potentially have.

Have a think about what you'll need when you go for a walk, or when shopping. For our money, we found the coffee cup holder useful for obvious reasons, a handlebar bag great for keeping our housekeys and phone close, and a seat liner invaluable for the occasional poo-splosion that occurred mid walk.

We didn't find a rain cover for the pram useful at all—if the weather looked bad, we just didn't go out—but in sunny Queensland, Australia, this wasn't often a problem. If you live in an area with unpredictable weather, or somewhere with just frankly terrible weather (we're looking at you, Scotland!) a rain cover might be essential. Similarly, if you live in the tropics it may be worth investigating mosquito covers, for bug protection without relying on insect repellent.

FINAL THOUGHTS

Unlike clothing, which in the early days may only fit a child for a few weeks, a good pram / stroller is something you will use every day for multiple years. It makes sense to spend money if you have it to get a good one, so that you end up with something you enjoy pushing.

If your budget is limited, consider buying second hand—yes you'll need to closely inspect the stroller before purchase, but it's usually pretty easy to see damage (check the wheels, check that the stroller folds and unfolds easily, and check for tears in the fabric). With a little bit of bargain shopping, you can often get expensive strollers that still look 'as new' for much better prices—and if you buy a stroller that doesn't end up working out for you or your family, you can always sell it second hand to recuperate some of the cost if you decide you wish to try another model.

Regardless of whether you buy new or second hand, put some thought and testing into what you end up purchasing. Going out for a walk with the bub really is a wonderful experience. For many parents, it can be the highlight of the day! Having a decent buggy helps make that happen.

FURTHER INFORMATION

How to Buy the Best Pram or Stroller for Your Baby (Web Article)
Focusing primarily on physical characteristics to look for (and avoid), this Choice.com.au article covers everything from safety features to comparisons between different styles of buggy. Importantly, the site is well regarded for its thorough product testing standards, so the commentary is written from a position of experience.

Stroller Safety: Tips for Parents (Web Article)
A slightly different take on the same topic, this Mayo Clinic article focuses less on physical features to look for

when buying a stroller, and more on practical tips to con-sider—such as the potential for where you live to affect your purchase.

Please see https://six-weeks.com/links#26 for web links.

27 | PRE-BABY PURCHASES

I think you need surprisingly little when you have a baby—just a place for them to sleep safely, a stroller, a car seat and some clothes. Don't *buy toys—you can't put them in the bed with baby anyway, and bub doesn't know what they are yet regardless! Toys will come later, and you may very-well be gifted secondhand items if your friends have kids ahead of yours anyway (babies can't tell the difference!).*

The one 'non-essential' thing I'd recommend is books—but make sure you like them, because you'll be reading them a million times. Babies can't really even see the pictures in books at first, but they can hear you. We read to Miguel from day one—I think that reading books helps you connect with a child.

STEPHANIE, MOTHER OF MIGUEL

Yes there are a lot of things you have to worry about after a baby is born, but there are also many items you can purchase ahead of time to make these first few weeks with a newborn that little bit easier.

The following list is not complete, but rather a smattering of some of the more important things to think about purchasing before your child is born. If you haven't yet had a baby shower, consider deciding what you want and then putting those items on a wish-list!

LOW VALUE ITEMS

You'll still need nappies, a cot, blankets and the rest, but here's a selection of basic necessities that you may not yet have thought about:

Bodysuits

Dependent on the weather where you live, your infant may spend most of their first six weeks in just a diaper and bodysuit (also sometimes called a wondersuit or onesie). These are like jumpsuits for babies—instead of separate shirt and pants, it's a one-piece outfit that lets you easily get a baby in and out. They come in both short and long-sleeve, with leg options to suit the season.

Because you probably won't leave the house much (the baby isn't immunized yet, and your body will need time to recover) you won't need fancy clothing beyond the occasional dress up for photos. A bunch of good bodysuits will be much more useful.

Look for a onesie with easy access to a baby's diaper—usually press studs at the bottom, or a zip down the front—as you'll be changing them a lot. Some suits also have clever overlapping folds or press-studs on the shoulders; these allow you to pull the suit down to get it off if it gets dirty rather than having to drag it over a baby's head. Chances are, you'll go through up to four or five suits a day as a result of diaper blowouts and vomit, so you can never have enough.

For us, 90% of our daughter's clothing in the first three months was second hand. Infants grow *fast* in these early days, sometimes only fitting into an item for one to two weeks, so hand-me-downs from friends were welcome—it isn't really 'well-used' if another baby has only worn it twice.

As a clothing-related side note: shoes for infants are pretty much useless until your child starts to walk, but socks or bodysuits with foot coverings can be useful to keep your baby's toes warm.

Some bodysuits also have fold out pouches on each hand that act like a glove. Hands should be uncovered for breastfeeding (so the child can locate and move to the nipple area, as well as knead the breast, which stimulates milk flow and increases maternal oxytocin levels[168]) but using bodysuits with gloves helps prevent young children scratching their faces at other times—infant fingernails can be sharp!

Sleep Suit

Nurses and midwives are masters of wrapping infants, but once you get home and have to do it yourself you'll find it harder than you think! A sleep suit (also called a sleep bag or swaddle) is a fantastic alternative to the traditional muslin cloth swaddle, and very easy to use. It's like a sleeping bag for babies which keeps their arms nice and tight so they don't startle and wake. It also lets you easily change your baby in the middle of the night without having to wake them as you unwrap and then re-wrap squares of cloth.

Our favorite brand of infant sleep suit is the *Swaddle Up* sleeping bag by Love to Dream[s] because its innovative sleeve system allows a baby to sleep with their arms in a more natural 'up' position than traditional sleep suits. It

---

[s] *For a link to their website, visit https://six-weeks.com/links#27*

means that the baby is not deprived of access to their hands for self-soothing, which may help them sleep longer, and it can be used from birth. The website is also incredibly easy to use.

Be sure that your sleep suit complies with infant hip safety requirements—suits that hold the infant's hips firmly together without allowing for free movement can predispose to hip dysplasia. Just because an infant wrap looks absolutely adorable with that matching headband doesn't mean it was designed with infant hip safety requirements in mind. The International Hip Dysplasia Institute has a brilliant website with lots of information and videos about hip dysplasia (and how to prevent it), and how to perform safe hip swaddling.[t]

Nursing Pillow

Nursing pillows, also called feeding pillows, are boomerang shaped cushions that new mothers can wrap around themselves when breastfeeding—the idea being that they help prop the baby within reach of a breast and take some of the weight from the mother's arms and upper back. They're also great when cuddling your baby and rocking her to sleep. Tiny babies may not seem heavy, but that will change after holding them for several hours!

---

[t] *Please visit https://six-weeks.com/links#27 for website details.*

Wheat Bag

Wheat bags, also sometimes called heat packs, are small satchels of various sizes made from corduroy, denim or a similar material. When put in the microwave for a *very* brief period of time, they can retain their heat for up to several hours.

A 12-inch-long bag can be useful because air-conditioning makes changing mats and beds *cold*. Some babies don't care about cool surfaces, but others scream—you won't know how your child reacts until he or she comes along.

In hospital, and then later in our home (our daughter was born mid-winter) we found pre-heating our child's bed and change table an essential part of keeping her calm and happy.

Of course, be careful when using wheat bags or any other sort of heating device around a baby. They have extremely sensitive skin, so you don't want surfaces to get too hot!

Whenever we used a wheat bag, we always tested it on ourselves first to make sure it wouldn't burn our daughter—even though the bag itself didn't come into contact with her (always remove the bag before you place your child down, as it's not safe to leave something like this beside your child).

Test the heat the same way you check the temperature of a baby bath—either with a thermometer or with the sensitive skin on the inside of your elbow. If the heat is too uncomfortable for your delicate skin, then *absolutely* don't use it to warm the bedding for your baby. Let it cool down to a temperature you can handle first.

Old-school Cloth Nappies

Before disposables became popular, babies where often wrapped in large white squares of terry toweling that were pinned on each side. You can still buy these cloth nappies from department stores, and our recommendation to purchase them here has nothing to do with a baby wearing them.

Cloth nappies are incredibly useful for mopping up spills, wiping up vomit and placing under a baby any time you want to do something like lay your child down on the floor (the one place a baby can't fall from!). Packs of cloth nappies—really just small, baby-sized white towels, when you think about it—are super cheap, easy to handle, easy to wash, easy to dry and easy to throw out and replace when required.

BATHING ITEMS

Bathtub

Nothing fancy required here—most of our parents probably bathed us in the kitchen sink, or a large clothes tub. But a dedicated baby bath will be useful as it's more portable (and you can also keep it more hygienic). There are plenty of products on the market these days and many are quite inexpensive.

One good option to consider is grabbing one with a drain plug, so you can just sit the bath over the kitchen sink and bathe the baby there, then drain it without having to worry about upending it to get all the water out—this is particularly important for mothers who have had a cesarean section and can't lift anything heavier than their infant for the first six weeks! If you have the money, consider collapsible tubs if you are low on storage space, or tubs with built-in stands if you're especially tall.

Note that while it's possible, bathing a newborn in your full-sized adult bath is usually more trouble than it's worth. Not only does it take an incredible amount of water to fill to a suitable level, but constantly bending so low to the ground (while supporting a baby) has the potential to put a huge strain on your back. Better to have a small plastic tub that you can sit on the kitchen sink or table at waist height.

Baby Bath Seat

Also called a baby bath support, these are devices that free up your hands and help keep an infant's head out of the water when they take a bath.

Remember, for much of the first few months (and in particular, the first six weeks) your child won't be able to lift their head, making bath time a backbreaking exercise of logistics. You'll need to keep their head out of the water as you try to wash them, and this cheap little device makes life sooo much easier. Make sure you get a newborn version, which looks a little like a tiny miniature sun lounger. After running the baby's bath and ensuring it is a correct temperature, you put this in the water so that the baby can lay on it. You'll still need to supervise your baby *very* closely, but it will eliminate constantly having to support their head, which saves your back.

You can also get something similar for the shower. Babies are slippery little morsels when they're wet and juggling them in the shower can be exceptionally difficult, not to mention dangerous if they accidentally slither from your grasp.

Baby towels

You'll want a minimum of two, because this is how many are required for each bath. The first will be to dry the baby, the second will be used immediately afterward when your baby is mostly dry to keep them warm (wet towels go cold very quickly).

Face Washers

Again, you'll want two: one to wash the baby's face and then butt (in that order!), and one to put over their tummy to keep them warm—the bath will most likely be so shallow that their stomach won't be submerged.

Bath thermometer

Yes, you can just test bath temperature with your elbow (it should feel comfortably warm, not hot, almost as if you can't notice the water at all). But if you like to get really exacting, look for a thermometer that floats on top of the water to constantly read the temperature (we have a cute yellow rubber ducky with a digital thermometer on its back) or a cheaper version that sticks to the side of the bath.

MORE EXPENSIVE ITEMS

Essentials for those with more money.

Baby Swing

It's funny—before having a child you don't think about such burning questions as 'when I really need to go to the toilet, what am I going to do with the baby?' Infant swings are a possible solution.

Sure, you can just put your child on the floor unattended (like we said earlier, you can't fall off a floor!) or in their bassinet, but for many infants, the gentle rocking of a swing can help keep a child happier for longer. If your child takes to it, swings will let you prepare dinner, have breakfast, put on the laundry and yes, go to the toilet, all while your child is safe and happy within eyesight.

There are several types of swing, including portable, manually operated, battery operated, and electric. Depending on your situation, consider getting an electric swing that plugs in, so you don't have to endlessly push the baby back and forth, and so you aren't constantly changing batteries. Note that different swings also rock different ways—some rock side to side, some rock head to toe, and some do both. If your baby doesn't enjoy one type of motion, they may enjoy the other.

If you do buy a swing, ensure it is suitable for new-borns and has appropriate head support. Unlike bassinets, swings are not designed for slumber—so if your infant falls asleep you can leave them in it for short periods, but not overnight without approval from a doctor. Additionally, the AAP recommends that parents limit the amount of awake time in a swing to prevent the baby's still-soft head from becoming flat as a result of being in the same position for too long.[169] Remember: swings aren't an all-day caretaking solution, but are instead 'a helpful pair of hands' when they're most needed.

Co-sleeper

Different infants prefer different sleeping arrangements, but what worked for our family was a co-sleeping bassinet, also sometimes called a side-car crib. This is a small cot that attaches to the side of the parent's bed, allowing the baby to sleep close to the mother its own safe sleeping environment. For women who are planning a cesarean, a co-sleeper may also be kinder to sore stomach muscles, as you won't have to get out of bed and bend over a cot to fetch your baby, but can rather just zip down the side-partition and then reach sideways to pull the baby close.

Digital Thermometer

Tympanic thermometers are expensive (compared to ordinary thermometers), but worth the price for their speed of use when a child is unwell. Just stick it in the ear, follow the instructions and -*boom!*- near instant temperature reading.

HIGH END ITEMS

Non-essential items that would make great group presents (or a gift from a very good friend!) at a baby shower.

SNOO

Quite possibly the most advanced infant bed on the market today, the SNOO was created by Dr. Harvey Karp, author of the *Happiest Baby* book series. Featuring a built-in swaddle, white noise function and sound-activated rocking function, the cot gently sways your baby to sleep so you don't have to, then settles her when she wakes in the middle of the night.

It isn't a miracle worker. If your baby is hungry, or sick, or just really, really doesn't want to sleep the SNOO can't magically make it happen. But the device does have a legion of devoted fans for a reason—it may help prolong sleep, and get your baby to sleep faster, resulting in more rest for exhausted parents.

Pram / Stroller / Buggy

Per the chapter on this item, it's worth getting a good quality stroller if you can. One way to do this is by deciding in advance what you want and putting it up as an option at a baby shower. If you can't decide, or would rather decide once you have your baby, consider asking for donations toward a gift voucher.

Car Seat

In many countries it is illegal to take your child in a car without a rearward-facing infant car seat. This means that unless you plan on walking home from the hospital, you'll need one prepped and ready before the baby is born. There are several different types of car seat on the market, but the two main ones are:

A *rearward only* facing car seat. These usually have a base which is secured to the car and a capsule system (where the child sits) which can be unclipped and removed from the car if required. They're great for taking a sleeping baby out of a car without waking them, and are also often able to be plugged into stroller travel systems (allowing you to take your sleeping bub from the car and put her straight into the pram, again without waking). It may also be possible to buy extra bases if you have multiple cars, so the one capsule can be clipped into whatever car you're using.

Because of their size, rearward only facing seats are always limited to a specific child age and weight, meaning you'll usually get around six months of use before you need to upgrade to something larger.

The second type of car seat you'll encounter is a *convertible* seat. These are initially installed to be rear facing and then later changed to forward facing as your child grows. These seats are often cheaper in the long run because you don't have to buy a new seat at around six months of age, but won't have the base-and-capsule system which allows parents to easily remove a sleeping baby from the car without waking.

In the end, the seat you choose is entirely up to your personal preference, and for many parents it comes down to price. With our child, we found the capsule system worthwhile, as resettling and putting a baby to sleep is so much harder than just unclipping a car seat and carrying the baby capsule-in-hand, inside. We were lucky enough to borrow the baby capsule from a friend whose own son had just been upgraded to a convertible seat.

Note that in many countries it's also possible to hire baby car seats, and this can be a cheaper option—rent a rearward facing capsule until your baby outgrows it, then purchase something larger. Another alternative can be to buy a second-hand car seat. If you are considering doing this, be sure to have the car seat properly checked to make sure it is structurally sound (in particular, check that it hasn't been in any car accidents before), that there are no parts that are missing or faulty, and that it still complies with the current safety standards for your state or country.

A sensible idea is to get the car seat professionally fitted. Car seats can be awkward to install, and the last thing you'll want to do is secure it incorrectly and put your baby's safety at risk. Many baby stores that have car seats for purchase will also have a professional installation service that may require a small fee. Other sources for professional installation include the emergency services (fire and ambulance services often have clinics that install child car seats and check them to ensure they're safe to use), or companies that specialize in professional car seat installation. If your car seat is professionally installed you should be given a certificate stating that this has happened. Sometimes you need this for an insurance claim if you are unlucky enough to have a car accident while your little bundle of joy is in the car.

FURTHER INFORMATION

Rear-Facing Car Seats for Infants & Toddlers (Web Article)
An article by the American Academy of Pediatrics with tips on purchasing and using car seats for newborns.

Please see https://six-weeks.com/links#27 for web links.

28 | STAYING POSITIVE

We made the decision for our mental health to leave the house as soon as possible. I think Luca was six days old at the time. The purpose of the excursion was to tell ourselves that we could still be normal people—who just happen to have a baby. We wanted to keep our identity in the face of this huge change that had happened in our lives.

We tried to make time to deliberately be the people we were before, at least in our own heads. It helped us think of our child as a gift that adds to our life, rather than a chore which took something away.

STEFANO, FATHER OF LUCA

Babies are wonderful, amazing little creatures. They can also be emotionally draining.

Even the best of us can falter when that first sleepless month turns into a second, or your child won't stop screaming, or you're having trouble breastfeeding. It can be hard to be positive sometimes.

There are, however, some proven, easy-to-do pearls of wisdom that may help lift your mood. Consider incorporating each of these ideas into your daily routine from the moment your child is born:

DON'T COMPARE

Every child is different. And every parent is different, too. Just because another child in your parent's group smiled a week ago, it doesn't mean there's anything wrong if your child isn't yet ready to smile themselves. Be wary of putting undue pressure on yourself and your baby.

And be wary of what you read online! That Instagram mommy blog you follow, where the parents are traveling the world with a two-week-old? Remember that's one photo—one second—out of twenty-four hours. And it probably took an hour to set up. Instagram, Pinterest and celebrity magazines are not real life. Don't compare yourself to them either.

Mummy blogs should also be approached with caution. Remember, there's no rule that bloggers or their responders *must* tell the truth about their own situation. If somebody swears black and blue that their newborn is already sleeping through the night, pooping rainbows or farting sunshine, they're probably telling fibs.

EXERCISE

It's so easy for people to say 'you need to exercise' when you've got a baby. But most of the self-righteous asshats sprouting that rubbish don't have a very young baby themselves. Exercise is *hard* with a baby. Seemingly impossible.

But… it is important. Exercise has so many proven benefits to mood and general health that unfortunately, the asshats are right. Even five minutes of aerobic exercise can initiate anti-anxiety effects within your body![170] and by now most people also know about the physical benefits.[171]

The question then, is not *if* you should exercise, but *how* to exercise when you've got a baby and all your time seems taken up with feeding, changing nappies and sleep.

The answer is to exercise *with* your baby. Think outside the box here—do squats as you're putting the baby to sleep over your shoulder, and calf raises while you change her diaper. Exercise is cumulative, so five minutes here and five minutes there can add up!

Gentle bicep curls using a newborn as the weight can be surprisingly effective, but perhaps easiest of all is to ensure you get your baby out of the house and take them for a stroll. Your baby will probably appreciate the change of scenery too! And who knows… the gentle sway of the pram or carrier as you walk may lull your little one to sleep.

PERFECT IS A MYTH

If you ever meet a parent who tells you their child is perfect, that they have eight hours sleep a night, that their house is clean and neat, that they started having sex again by day four or that they've never sat on the floor sobbing, wondering what they got themselves into—they're either lying or they've got a full time nanny.

Don't try to be perfect—it's impossible. You're not Mary Poppins—and you know what? Your child doesn't care. She doesn't know that you feel like you've got no idea what you're doing. She just wants to be kept safe, held close, and fed.

LET IT GO

Again, your baby doesn't care if the dishes are dirty, the laundry's not done every day, or even if you're too tired to shower. Let it go. Find happiness in that extra hour of sleep.

OUTSOURCE

If you have friends close at hand, this is one of the easiest things you can do to make life with a baby just that little bit simpler. Ask those you know and love for help with the yardwork, cleaning, groceries and childcare duties. Most people are happy to help! In fact, most people want to, they just don't know how... so don't be scared to ask them for help with specific tasks.

If you have extra cash, there're even more things you can do. Many busy working couples employ night nurses or nannies to take some of the pressure off, and there's already a whole lot of new parents out there using meal services right now so they don't have to worry about cooking. If the budget in your house is tight, pre-plan before the baby arrives and cook extra serves with every meal that you can then freeze. If you already have your baby, ask friends to cook up a batch of food! Then put it in the freezer to give you options later.

FOCUS ON THE POSITIVES

When you're down in the dumps it can be hard to remember that there're good things that come from having a baby—in fact, many more positive things than negatives, when all's said and done. So make a list! And you're allowed to be a little silly. Watching a lot of TV while you put the baby to bed each night? Write that down. Think it will be pretty cool to have a mini-me of your very own to train? Write that down too. Looking forward to that first smile? It will come—make a note of it so you know why you're doing all this hard work.

TALK TO SOMEONE

Don't bottle it up. There're a whole lot of other people in the same situation, and a whole lot of people that were previously where you are now but survived and came through unscathed. Talking to friends, relatives, your partner or a counselor can help put things in perspective, give you valuable tips that will make your life easier and importantly—let other people know what's going on, so they can try and help.

FURTHER INFORMATION

25 Ways to Handle the Stress of a New Baby (Web Article)
Sensible, practical advice from psychologists and a parenting coach about things that might help reduce the stress many new parent's experience.

Websites & Emergency Contact Numbers (Fact Sheet)
Organized by country, this page gives a list of local websites and organizations that are here to help with a variety of mental health issues, including depression.

Please see https://six-weeks.com/links#28 for web links.

29 | REAL ADVICE

Everyone has an opinion.

But that doesn't mean everyone is right.

JIM, FATHER OF ETHAN

To close out the book, this chapter will be a little different from the others. Information within it isn't research based, it's something that is perhaps even better—real advice from real parents.

All too often, mothers, fathers and caregivers put a stupid façade over their life, saying that 'everything is fine' and 'babies aren't hard.' This can be damaging. So, in this chapter, we wanted to be honest. To admit that parenting can be hard, and that the first six weeks, for many parents, are the hardest.

Family, friends and complete strangers were asked one simple question: If you could give any advice to new parents about the first six weeks, what would you say?

You may notice that some of the advice is conflicting. This is intentional. The purpose of this chapter is not to give you evidence-based advice. *It's to show you that every single baby, and every experience, is different.* If you find wisdom or a helpful tip in someone's comments, all the better.

Strong language warning ahead!

When your partner goes back to work, let them have half an hour when they come back in the door each night (if you can). Sometimes we forget, because they've been away all day, that they've been working too! It stops burnout and makes taking back the kid a joy, not a chore.

Anonymous, recovery nurse. Mother of three.

Ha! Everything and every theory you read about newborns goes out the door in the first six weeks. You can read about attachment theory and completely fail at it because your crazy hormones are out of sorts and the cry of your newborn baby beats all logical thinking. *That's ok.*

Accept that things will not go as planned no matter how much you try, and forgive yourself for sleeping through feeding time if it happens. Every baby is unique and your experience will be too. Don't compare and trust your gut BUT most of all no matter how hard it is, it will end!

My child is now five, and I forget that sometimes I sat in the bathroom crying from exhaustion, frustration and confusion. Good luck!

Griselda, therapist. Mother of one

Lock yourself and your baby away for the first 6 weeks to avoid any illness and unnecessary advice from other people. Gives mum and dad time to really connect and understand their baby's needs.

Best thing I ever did.

Ashlyn, registered nurse and midwife. Mother of
Adelaide Grace

Ooh boy, the first six weeks seem like a lifetime ago—my eldest turns 18 in two months! My best advice would be to deal with sleep, food, and wet nappies. Everything else can wait. If anyone cares that your dishes aren't done or that you're wearing the same t-shirt three days in a row, ignore them.

Lucie, writer. Mother of two

So, the first six weeks were rough. My milk supply wasn't what I hoped it to be. I didn't realize it could take up to three days for my milk supply to come in, and Tommy (our child) was starving—so he was unsettled and woke frequently.

I struggled for a couple of weeks, pumping like crazy, but it didn't help. I remember Steve and I going to a maternity clinic (I feel like we lived there) and discussing my issues with breastfeeding. I desperately wanted to make it to six months for the immunity benefits but didn't think I could.

Each time I asked if I could switch to formula (funny, when I look back on it, that I felt I needed to ask for permission) the midwives kept talking me out of it. They'd just say 'keep going' and telling me 'breast is best' like it was some sort of mantra. By this stage I was crying, Tommy was crying, and thank God Steve eventually put his foot down. "My son is starving. We're going to mix feed," he said, before bundling us into the car to buy a tin of formula.

I was so relieved. Tommy became more settled and slept a little better—not perfect, but at least now he didn't scream after every meal. It felt like I was feeding on the hour, including overnight!! Sleep was a little luxury at that stage.

Then somewhere between four to six weeks I developed postnatal depression. It was more than the baby blues—I just couldn't stop crying. I'd cry Tommy to sleep. I was trying my absolute hardest, I knew he needed more (comfort) but I had no physical or emotional energy.

Luckily (?) I had suffered depression before so knew what it was. I got help—and thank goodness I did. At the time it felt like there was no hope left, but with the right medication and therapy I got through that dark tunnel and out the other side.

To any other mothers that have PND, remember it's not a weakness, just an illness. You wouldn't be ashamed of seeking help for a broken arm. Don't be ashamed of seeking help for depression, either.

As far as tips for new parents, here's a couple of things that people don't tell you:

Bottles: I just picked a brand and got lucky it worked. But some babies have trouble with bottles, so experiment with different types if you need to.

Dummies: There are so many different types to choose from, and so much pressure on whether to have one or not—though with an unsettled baby, it was a no-brainer for us. Our midwife said the old-school cherry shaped ones were the best, but Tommy hated them. I chose an age appropriate orthodontic one and he thankfully took to it. So again, experiment if you need to.

Diapers: Do you go cloth vs. disposable? I felt societal pressure to 'do the right thing' and get cloth, but just didn't have the energy to add more pressure on myself with the upkeep of extra washing & sanitizing. Do what's right for your family and ignore the haters.

Medication: After seeing a doctor with a special interest in lactation medicine and breastfeeding, I was put on meds to increase my supply. This helped a little, but I should have stopped at four months and didn't, getting subsequent gastrointestinal issues from prolonged use. Luckily these resolved quickly, but they just prove that it's important to follow the advice of your doctor, even if you think that sometimes you know better!

Advice: Take all 'well meaning' advice with a grain of salt (unless it's from a doctor!). You'll get a lot of opinions from friends, family and random strangers. It can be overwhelming. Choose what's best for you and your baby.

Nappy Rash: The best advice we were given was to slather the baby's butt with Vaseline or Sudocream. It helps to act as a barrier and protect their skin from those initial quite harsh poos.

Umbilical Cord: You will come home with a partial umbilical cord attached to your child, clamped. It's kinda gross but will one day accidentally fall off when knocked. Be prepared for that.

You will not have all the answers—no one does. Make all decisions to the best of your knowledge at the time and enjoy your precious little one. The first six weeks go by way too quickly. Good luck on your journey.

Clare, nurse. Mother of Thomas

First, all mums should be given a Haakaa[u] before they leave hospital. Second, everyone knows about the food

---

[u] *A haakaa is a portable hand pump that is highly regarded by many mothers. You can find a link to the website at https://six-weeks.com/links#29.*

you can't eat while pregnant, but no one tells you about food to avoid when breastfeeding! Make sure you do some research on this if you've decided to go this route when feeding your baby.

Amanda. Mother of two

Leave the house at least once a day - to take Bub for a walk, even if just around the block or to get a coffee. Fresh air and a little exercise helps clear the head!

Ben, senior sales executive. Father of two

Most cultures have advice on what to eat to help your milk come in, but that did not seem true of my American friends when we were all having babies. Do some research.

Nobody tells you that one day the milk just shows up and your boob is as hard as a boulder (run your thumb down the milk ducts to help express the milk when your baby is nursing), that some newborns are in fact terrible at nursing and you have to teach them how to do it!

Also strangely, one kid of ours cried every time we changed his diaper. Turns out he needed the wipe warmer. The other kid didn't.

Julia, author. Mother of two

Oh gosh where to begin. Hmmmm.

Let go of expectations. Get help with meals and washing. Stop trying to be perfect or comparing your baby or parenting style to others.

Take a moment for yourself. It's ok to feel helpless, tired, and to cry. The first six weeks are such a beautiful time, but they can also be soul destroying.

The joys of sharing wee and poo photos will take your relationship to new levels—and breast feeding was such a hurdle! The first real smiles, finding yourself able to settle a bubba and later seeing them wake is heaven.

Ellen, presenter. Mother of one

My first tip is re: midwives.

As new parents we deferred to everyone, but we definitely listened to the midwives more than we should have. Their expertise extends to babies being born, but once they are out, a midwife is just another person with an opinion (albeit one that is strongly held and generally contradictory to everything else you get told).

By the time we worked this out my wife had sustained damage through trying to feed our little girl with a tongue tie and it set feeding back weeks. It was painful, distressing, and absolutely avoidable.

My second tip is to go and see the community health nurses and find one that you like, they're an amazing resource and were super helpful at getting us back on track and calming our nerves!

The good news is that the tough times do pass, and then the magical times begin. I can still remember the moment when I realized why people go back for more!

Michael, PHD candidate and father of Chloe

Lactation consultants are worth their weight in gold! Also, mums that need to pump to be able to feed should get themselves a double pump and cut holes in an old bra so that they're hands free.

Breastfeeding isn't easy for everyone. While for some it comes naturally, for others both mum and bub may have to learn how to do it well. My bub didn't latch until he was five weeks old and even then I had to wear a nipple shield for him to be able to feed until he was four months old.

Sally, ex-Disney princess. Mother of Ethan

It's super tough in the beginning especially if you are predisposed to being a bit 'Type A'. What I've learned is that you should feed your kid. Who cares whether it's breast milk or formula or a mixture of both. If I stayed on the pumping schedule given to me by the lactation specialist... I would have gone mad. He's 7 months now and is not behind in his developmental milestones despite having been fed ½ formula and ½ breast milk.

Also, give yourselves a break. Accept help and get out when you can. Getting out at least once a day saved me (either with or without the kid) because let's face it... it's super fun to have a newborn but it can also be repetitive.

Lastly, I wouldn't trade any of it. Cuddles are not overrated. Snuggle with that kid every chance you get.

Mae, doctor. Mother of one

The biggest thing for me was not realizing both you AND baby have to learn how to breastfeed. When Luciana was born they latched her the first few times for me. But they didn't show ME how to do it.

After a day or two I had the lactation consultant come in and thank GOD I did. Changed everything for the positive and I kept in touch with her off and on for the first six weeks to make sure all was ok. She really helped me so much.

Also, I knew I'd be tired, but I had NO CLUE how tired. I gave myself grace and dropped all other expectations of myself other than healing and tending to the baby. Those first six weeks and even on to the first three months are dark but there is light at the end of the tunnel.

Ask for help when you need it, remember this too shall pass, and try to soak up as much as you can. Don't stress about the baby getting "used" to only sleeping on you... eventually they will sleep on their own too. Soak up those infant cuddles. There is nothing like them in the world!

Crystal. Mother of two

Routine, routine, routine, live and die by it!

I bottle fed from birth which was *the* best choice for myself and my children. 4-hour feeds from birth, no cluster feeding, and my babies were fuller longer so slept solidly.

Thinking children will magically sleep through at some point is dangerous. This is not guaranteed and there sure as hell isn't an age this kicks in. Almost three years in and we're still not there.

And sleep when the baby sleeps is bullshit! When will the laundry, cleaning, groceries, bottles etc. get done?

Best piece of wisdom: the first 10 weeks are survival, just keep everyone alive. If you can afford it get a healthy food delivery service so you eat, but don't have to live on take out. Also get professional photos during these weeks. You won't take enough photos yourself, you're too busy.

Meredith, CEO. Mother of two

I had two kids, both totally the opposite. One was a nightmare for the first few months, waking up every 40 min sleep cycle, the other was a piece of cake. Two years later... they are still very opposite! So I guess a lot of how the first six weeks go for a new parent is down to random luck.

No matter what all the sleep experts say, if you have a bad sleeper, there's not much you can do about it. The hardest thing about lack of sleep? Work colleagues who are only slightly annoying normally... I just wanted to stab them!

Jason, engineer. Father of two

Tip one is a simple one—each child is different. My daughter is the polar opposite to my son. She slept from 7pm to 7am from week one, but my son who is four has not slept a full night yet.

Tip two is to do what's right for your child. Don't care what others think! For example, both our children were bottle fed (my wife had medical issues which made breast feeding not an option). The judgment from other mothers was unbelievable.

As long as you love your child you will always do the right thing.

Brad, hotelier. Father of two

Just take your time, one step at a time, one day at a time. This process is a learning curve. It will put you through your paces as a parent, mother, dad and couple. You're just learning how to navigate, be flexible, be forgiving and be kind to each other.

Things might pop up that you never thought would be a problem or a difficulty. Communication is key, here. Parenting is rough for the first one to two years, not just the first six weeks. Give yourself permission to re-evaluate what your parenting style is. It may be completely different to your partner's and if so, try to meet each other in the middle.

All this said though, a rough start in the beginning as well as sleep deprivation and exhaustion are completely normal for all parents, so hang in there!

Danielle, mother of two

Don't listen to advice from older people. Listen to your friends who are new parents, but not last generation mums, who may be well-meaning but also outdated.

Ellainne, retired. Mother of Lauren and Kate[v]

---

[v] Thanks mum! *Kate*

A few things spring to mind:

1. For females - loss of identity. Coming from a senior corporate role "where I knew my shit" to "do I put a jumper on the baby or not" is both confusing, frustrating and overwhelming. It will take time to get into the swing of being a stay at home mum.

2. We had a 36-hour labor followed by an emergency cesarean. You start off tired and then become overtired which makes it hard to sleep. Sleep when the baby sleeps is good advice but can be difficult to put into practice.

3. If your baby doesn't sleep, you're not a failure as a parent. Same goes for breast vs. bottle. It makes zero difference.

4. Before the baby is born, attend counseling as a couple. You may think you're on the same page but often you're not. Sleep deprivation does strange things to your body (male and female).

5. If having a baby shower, ask people to buy you a week's worth of food delivery for when the baby arrives.

6. Males or the other parent / caregiver can feel helpless. Before the baby is born, consider how they will help.

7. Trust yourself. If you think something is wrong, find someone who will listen to you. Our daughter had an

undiagnosed medical problem for the first 7 months of her life. Symptoms included sleeping in 30-minute blocks every 2 hours day and night, then waking up screaming, neck stiffness, latching issues (not enough food and too much air), and screaming in the car seat (she was in pain from the position and mouth deformity. As she was in constant pain, she needed to be held a lot. We were dismissed by 8 medical professionals until a sleep consultant diagnosed the problem (sigh).

8. Night sweating is real for some people. Don't freak out, it's normal!

9. You can't cuddle a baby too much.

10. Be prepared to do stupid shit. I point my car keys at the front door to try and open it :p

11. Your baby only knows your way. You're the best and only parents it has. In its eyes, you're perfect.

Lindsay, HR professional. Mother of Billie

I had a really hard time adjusting to life with my first. She screamed all the time and I thought my life was over. I couldn't do anything and she hated the car... so that made going anywhere miserable. People only tell you how wonderful having a child is... they don't tell you all the hard stuff that comes with it. So, some words of advice:

Ask for help. Don't go through it alone. For a woman dealing with hormone changes, that can be extremely difficult. I found it helpful to have visitors constantly. They were a source of comfort and someone to talk to. It also was amazing to hand off the baby and take a break when I needed it.

If you're having one of those days when the baby just won't stop screaming, walk away from her. As long as she's safe and just needs to scream, walk outside by yourself for a little bit to take a breather and regroup.

Remember this... even though it feels like it will, this will NOT last forever. This is just a short phase, and it's only going to get better and better (I promise). I've had a blast with my daughter over the last six years... it's all totally worth it!!

As a side note, I just had a son three months ago. I was scared of this whole infant stage again. Luckily this time around has been a lot better so far... fingers crossed that continues. Good luck and enjoy your newborn baby. She won't be small forever xo

Sandra, teacher. Mother of Chloe and Joseph

Everyone has an opinion about how to parent. Take what resonates with you and remember that the rest of it is crap.

Elderly relatives may remember a time when giving babies alcohol to "help" with sleep / colic / everything was just what you did. It was bad then, and it's bad now. Most advances from 10+ years ago have been superseded.

Also, tell people to do your laundry or fuck off. There should be no visitors, only people doing essential work that you are too busy for.

Finally, if in doubt, see a doctor—babies get sick fast. If you're worried you need to check, even if you checked yesterday or that morning. No one will mind. Better safe than sorry.

Laura, social work student. Mother of
Evan, Stas, Troy and Victor

Those first six weeks are pretty tough. Such a steep learning curve. I still remember leaving the hospital in disbelief that they were letting us leave the hospital with a real baby!!

One piece of advice is never feel like you can't ask someone else for help or guidance. Whether it be a close friend, mother, aunt or a random lady at the end of the breastfeeding helpline at 2am. The more you ask, the closer you'll get to something that will work.

Also, after having two girls, the phrase "the nights/days are long but the years are short" is so true. The nights without sleep felt like they'd never end but now 7 years have passed since I had my first, and it feels like a blink of an eye.

Cindy, teacher. Mother of Grace and Sophie

Seeing my child for the first time was fantastic, though the thoughts that come rushing to you! What's the next step? Is my wife ok and is she going to be ok?

I found the first six weeks eye opening, fun, life changing, scary, stressful and most importantly, *everything felt out of my control.*

As the guy, you don't know if you're doing the right thing for your partner and newborn. You sit and watch your wife trying to handle it, but you yourself are limited in how you can help. It's stressful and as a guy I felt helpless and started to get depressed (PND is real for guys).

The most important way I was able to help, in the end, turned out to be just 'being there' for my partner—a rock she could cry on, shout at, push away and pull back as she went through her own journey.

The biggest thing I learned in the first six weeks was not to bottle your feelings up. Find someone—even if it is not your partner—to chat to. It helps. Trust me, I left it nearly too late and it tore me apart, but once I worked up to talk, I was better for it.

The first six weeks (and the rest of it), is hard—but worth all the struggle of it for the new addition in my life.

Paul, manager. Father of Tilda

For the first 6 weeks, you are recovering. So, take advantage of that. Have a comfy chair, water and snacks, put your feet up and feed, feed, feed. Let baby sleep on you if they want, as you cannot 'spoil' a baby by holding them too much. And you cannot overfeed a breastfed baby. Feed your baby to sleep, don't worry about a messy house, don't obsess over your baby's sleeping habits.

Nothing 'can't wait.' They are only newborns for such a short time so take every day as it comes, and know that whatever issue you are having today, will pass. Believe it or not, one day you will wish that you could just have one more day with them as a newborn.

I loved breastfeeding. But it didn't start out easy for me at all. In fact, the pain initially was excruciating.

I was always told it should not hurt. *I totally disagree.* For me, it was incredibly painful. During this time, I saw a lactation consultant many times and called the Breast-feeding Association between appointments. Nothing was wrong with the latch—the baby was gaining weight—but the pain for the first six weeks continued. I used shields, I used copious amounts of nipple cream, wore breast shells in between feeds, and pumped in between feeds then fed that through a bottle to give myself a break.

Then at the six-week mark, it magically stopped hurting. I continued to feed until my eldest self-weaned at 22 months.

Second time around, I told myself I wasn't going to allow the new baby to cause damage from the start. So when he was born, if feeding hurt, I took him off and relatched—many times, until it no longer made my toes curl. The pain stopped this time within two weeks.

I guess the moral is, even with years of successful breastfeeding under my belt, I still felt pain for the first two weeks with my second child. So when you are told breastfeeding shouldn't hurt, that doesn't mean it *can't,* even if everything is being done right. Seek advice from a lactation consultant. Everyone is different.

The final piece of advice I have for new mums is when you return from being out, repack your baby bag immediately. When you do need to leave the house again, it's one less thing to remember!

Ronwyn, Events Specialist. Mother of Jay and Liam

Navigating your way through the first 6 weeks or so with your first baby is incredibly daunting. Your body is recovering from the physical trauma of birth (even if it was a generally positive experience), you are sleep-deprived and vulnerable, everyone is offering you often conflicting advice, you are being regularly poked and prodded like a farm animal by midwives/medical professionals and meanwhile you are responsible for keeping a tiny human being alive. If you are lucky, you have a loving but also sleep-deprived and vulnerable partner to help make your way through the fog.

Looking back, my second and third births and the weeks following were so much more positive than my first. I wish that I had known the first time around about the importance of staying relaxed (I spent far too much time feeling anxious about the pain of birth), the benefits of regular pregnancy yoga and breathing, and the value of resting at home with your newborn in the first month as much as possible and not having too many visitors or trying to do too much. During my next pregnancy, I went on a Calm Birth course—which I would highly recommend to anyone—to help understand the process of birth (which helped me to not feel so anxious) and learn techniques for staying relaxed. The course completely transformed my attitude to birth and helped me stay in a positive frame of mind.

I struggled to fully breastfeed with each of my babies. The first time around was the most challenging, as I couldn't understand why my baby wasn't putting on weight. The midwives were telling me to keep breastfeeding and insisted that that would boost my supply, strongly advising against using formula. And yet my baby would not stop crying, and no amount of feeding or pumping or motilium or fenugreek or protein powder or lactation cookies would improve the situation. It was only when a friend suggested mixed feeding that I realized there was another way, and I didn't look back.

To this day, I still feel angry that not one of the midwives recommended formula when in retrospect my baby was obviously not getting enough milk and crying with hunger, and it took a few long and stressful weeks of muddling through for me to understand this. Formula shouldn't be frowned on—fed is best. I successfully mix fed each of my babies for 6 months before switching completely to formula, but I still feel terrible for effectively starving/dehydrating my baby in those first few weeks!

I was very set on a routine from 3 months onwards. I wish now that I had given him more cuddles when settling in those early months, and used a co-sleeping mattress which made nighttime breastfeeding so much easier and safer, as we did with our second and third.

Finally, batch cook as much as possible before baby is born so that you have lots of meals in the freezer, and make the most of online grocery shopping!

In a nutshell, I wish someone had told me to:

- stay relaxed
- do pregnancy yoga
- rest at home as much as possible in the first month
- don't delay using formula if you need it
- give your baby lots of cuddles
- plan ahead for meals, and
- use a co-sleeping mattress if it keeps you sane!

Siân, communications professional. Mother of
Edward, Thomas and Freya

When giving babies daytime naps, put a crib in the living room/kitchen (somewhere busy and noisy) and they sleep much better as they are used to people being around while in the womb. Quiet bedrooms are alien to what they are used to. Also doing this helps them sleep in noisy places later on in life. My child is now 14 and can sleep anywhere.

Chris, IT Specialist. Father of Brooke

As a first-time mum there's an overload of info out there, and because it's all new it puts a lot of stress and doubt in one's mind. What I did for my first child I did the opposite with my second. People say you know when they're hungry or tired by their 'signs.' I had no idea with my first, but with my second it was clear as day, so don't worry—it all just takes time!

Lisa, Mother of two

As a mum of two my biggest learning is that a mother's instinct is *always* right. Never let anyone tell you otherwise. Sure, sometimes we need to try what books or people tell us, but that gut instinct that mums have about their babies/children is precious. If your heart says to cuddle them, cuddle them. If your heart says to leave them for a few minutes, leave them. Also, you can't hug a baby too much. They need to be close to us. If I knew when my babies were little what I know now—I'd babywear with a soft carrier and hold them much more than I did.

Sonia, consultant. Mother of two

30 | FINAL WORDS

No one tells you how tough life is with a newborn. Hopefully after reading this book you'll understand it a little better—not because we want to scare you, but because information is power, and a little foreknowledge can make the transition to parenthood that much easier.

For some, being a parent is easy right from the very start… and for others it's not.

In the end, it really doesn't matter. What's most important is that your child grows up healthy, happy and loved. So hang in there—you'll be an amazing parent!

It might help to keep in mind that while the first six weeks can seem like Groundhog Day, there will be a time—just around the corner—where the developmental milestones come thick and fast.

Soon your child will smile for the first time, and then giggle, and then all of a sudden one after another and not-in-any-particular-order she'll discover her hands and reach for objects and blow bubbles and stick out her tongue and track you with her eyes!

And all these things will be mind-blowing as a parent. It's the moments like these that make it all worth it.

Hopefully this book has helped your transition. Having read it, you won't know everything... but if you know just a little more, and feel just that bit more prepared... we'll have done our job.

Best of luck on this most amazing of journeys.

Kate + alich

APPENDIX 1: SOCIAL MEDIA POST

On the next page is a short blurb that some parents have found helpful for announcing their return from hospital. Feel free to modify as required to suit what you feel is most important, and use on Facebook, Instagram, stick it to the front door or put anywhere else you wish:

We are home with our beautiful child! Please understand we have worked very hard to create our darling infant and wish to take every measure to protect them. A healthy home is a happy home. We appreciate your understanding and support in making this happen.

If you're planning on visiting, we ask that you make sure you are up to date with your vaccinations, especially Whooping Cough and the Flu. If you can't or choose not to be vaccinated, that is also OK, our child will look forward to meeting you after her six-week vaccinations.

If you or anyone in your family have the sniffles or a cough please wait until you're well again to visit.

Lastly, please respect how special this family time is as we are learning all about our beautiful child—please keep your visits short and sweet and understand that we're very excited but also very tired.

Thank you for your love and support.

An electronic copy of this post for you to copy and paste can be found at https://six-weeks.com/links#A1

APPENDIX 2: RECOMMENDED RESOURCES

You can find links to all recommended resources online at https://six-weeks.com/links#A2

Mesmerised (Book)

A fun, beautiful book to stimulate infants with silhouettes and basic shapes.

Raising Children (Website)

A favorite recommendation of Australian paediatricians, the Raising Children Website is an amazing resource for new parents. It has easy to find articles on a variety of baby related topics and the best thing is, everything on the site is evidence-based and verified by experts.

Your 6-Week-Old Baby's Development (Web Articles)
These six articles make a great 'cheat sheet' that give you the basics of everything from developmental milestones to sleep and nutrition during the first six weeks, with handy infographics for those not into heavy reading.

The First 12 Weeks of Your Little One's Life (Web Articles)
Another great, short, week-by-week description of your baby, this time up to 12 weeks. It contains bite-sized chunks of knowledge for you to digest about what your child is experiencing *right now*, and what you can expect from them developmentally (just remember that every baby is different, and all milestones are guidelines only!).

Your Guide to the First 12 Months (PDF)
Developed by the Queensland Health Children's Hospital and Health Service, we had a midwife recommend this

document to us and it's great! Extending beyond six weeks and into the first year, it discusses (in broad brushstrokes) issues such as bonding, breastfeeding, formula feeding, sun protection and more. Though the document is for Australian audiences, it's relevant for any child.

Cribsheet (Book)

There are a lot of claims about how to correctly parent your child. Emily Oster examines the data behind many of them to give fact-based advice on a number of important topics, including breastfeeding, sleep training and milestones.

Though this book is full of facts and figures, Cribsheet is a surprisingly fun and easy read! If you're the sort of person who likes to know *why* people are telling you to do something (and if their advice is correct) this book is well worth investigating. Anxious parents may also gain benefit from this book through its clear, data driven statements about what's important to worry about, and what's not.

The Data-Driven Parenting Book You Need (Web Article)
Not sure about Cribsheet? This is a great, free 'taster article' if you're undecided as to whether the book is for you. Among other things, it discusses the book's opinion on drinking alcohol while breastfeeding, crying it out as a training technique and when to potty train. It's a nice, fun, easy read.

All About Newborn Senses (Web Article)
Founded by an evolutionary anthropologist, the 'about' page of parentingscience.com says it all:

"I've got opinions. But who cares? You might be a scientist, physician, or teacher. Maybe you're an educated, skeptical layperson who loves science. Whatever the case, you don't need a sermon. You need evidence. You can draw your own conclusions."

This is an amazing, data-backed page explaining all about what a newborn can see, hear, touch and smell. There's no advice, just plenty of rich, interesting facts for you to soak up about your little baby.

Baby Doctor Mamas (Podcast)

Hosted by two female pediatricians, this is Kate's favorite baby related podcast and a great way to keep yourself entertained and informed when your hands are full and you find yourself unable or unwilling to read. Episodes discuss everything from baby breathing patterns to breast pumps and co-sleeping to colic, with links to further information for everything discussed on the show.

Baby Love (Book)

593 pages long and so heavy you could wrap it in swaddles and call it an infant, Robin Barker's Baby Love is a definitive compendium of baby related knowledge, with information on everything from identifying different skin rashes, to how to cut tiny fingernails, to bottle sterilization techniques. The book isn't exactly 'light reading,' but it's great for consulting when you have a specific question.

Note that Baby Love is written for an Australian market, meaning all measurements are in metric (not imperial),[w] however the book is still very worthwhile for those

---

[w] *Technically there is a US edition, however due to issues with the publisher it has not been updated since 2002. We recommend purchasing the AU edition.*

Americans out there willing to convert *Celsius* to *Fahrenheit* and *grams* to *ounces* (that's what Google is for, right?).

Pulling up the Drawbridge (Blog Article)
It's okay not to be a Super Mom after the birth of your child. And it's okay just to slow down for a little while, pull up the drawbridge and look after yourself and your baby first—before the cleaning, shopping, visiting and million other things clamoring for attention in your new life.

The Wonder Weeks (Book)
If you enjoyed or were intrigued by the chapter on Wonder Weeks, you may enjoy this book. It contains explanations and coping strategies for each of the 10 leaps discussed in the book, making tracking your child's progress through the wonder weeks a breeze.

The Happiest Baby Guide to Great Sleep (Book)

Intelligent, practical advice on how to get your child to sleep better, with chapters for dealing with newborns all the way up to toddlers. Dr. Karp's '5 S' technique, from this book, is described on the chapter on *How to calm a crying baby*.

TinyBeans (App)

Think of the TinyBeans app (and accompanying website) as an invite-only 'Facebook for Babies.' You put up photos whenever you want and then only people you've authorized can see them.

It's a great way to share special moments with close friends and family, especially those who live long distance, while still keeping your family moments (and your child's photos) private. The app's simple calendar system means that people can log in whenever they want—every day, or once a month—and quickly catch up on what they've missed.

The free version of the app is excellent, or you can pay a small yearly fee for slightly more features.

Baby Bliss (Book)

Another book by Dr. Karp, this one focusing specifically on infants 3 months and younger, including information about calming reflexes and developing night-time sleep habits.

Surviving the First Six Weeks! (Book)

Yes this is shameless self-promotion, but... if you found this book helpful, interesting and most importantly useful, why not buy it for someone else that's about to have a baby?

Sometimes it can be hard to tell prospective parents what life with a young child is really like. No-one wants to say 'hey it's hard' in the face of all that excitement. A book about what life is *really* like can be a positive way to help parents without damaging that all-important friendship or looking like you're raining on the prospective new parent's parade.

Tip: Second-hand Books

Because many books about children are age specific (this one is a great example!) the savvy shopper will find many great bargains at charity and second-hand stores—no matter how invaluable a book has been, its use will decrease as the child grows past it!

Make sure you check charity shops out before making expensive purchases, but do your research before buying. With your phone, look up the latest edition online vs. the one in your hand to ensure it isn't out of date. Doing this can save you hundreds of dollars!!

ENDNOTES

Links to all online resources can be found at
https://six-weeks.com/links

---

[1] "Language Development: Speech Milestones for Babies." *Mayo Clinic*, Mayo Foundation for Medical Education and Research, 7 Mar. 2019. (link available)

[2] "When Will My Baby Smile for the First Time?" *BabyCenter Australia*. (link available)

[3] "0-1 Month: Newborn Development." *Raising Children Network*, 13 Mar. 2020. (link available)

[4] Karp, Harvey. *The Happiest Baby on the Block: the New Way to Calm Crying and Help Your Baby Sleep Longer*. Bantam Books, 2002, p. 8-9

5   Karp, Harvey. *The Happiest Baby on the Block: the New Way to Calm Crying and Help Your Baby Sleep Longer*. Bantam Books, 2002, p. 8-9

6   "Baby Weight Losses and Weight Gains." *Australian Breastfeeding Association*, Jan. 2019. (link available)

7   "Monitoring Your Newborns Weight Gain." *American Pregnancy Association*, Aug. 2015. (link available)

8   "Is My Baby Getting Enough Milk?" *Australian Breastfeeding Association*, Aug. 2017. (link available)

9   Heinrichs, Markus, et al. "Selective Amnesic Effects of Oxytocin on Human Memory." *Physiology & Behavior*, Elsevier, 20 Oct. 2004, vol 83, p. 31-38. (link available)

10 Abraham, Eyal, et al. "Fathers Brain Is Sensitive to Childcare Experiences." *Proceedings of the National Academy of Sciences*, vol. 111, no. 27, 27 May 2014, pp. 9792–9797., doi:10.1073/pnas.1402569111. (link available)

11 "Newborn Sleep: What to Expect." *Raising Children Network*, 17 May 2019. (link available)

12 "How Often to Breastfeed." *Sutter Health*. (link available)

13 Masters, Maria. "When Will Your Baby Sleep Through the Night?" *What to Expect*, 28 Feb. 2020. (link available)

14 "Infant Sleep." *Stanford Children's Health - Lucile Packard Children's Hospital Stanford*. (link available)

15 Karp, Harvey. "'Wake & Sleep': Teaching Babies to Sleep on Their Own." *Happiest Baby Australia*, 9 Aug. 2015. (link available)

16 Hall, Tizzie. "Baby Comforters: Comfort (for Baby) and Joy (for Parents)." *Save Our Sleep*. (link available)

17 St. James-Roberts, Ian. "Preventing and Managing Infant Sleep Problems." *The Period of Purple Crying*, Dec. 2013. (link available)

18 "Helping Babies Sleep and Settle: 0-6 Months." *Raising Children Network*, 20 May 2019. (link available)

19 Powell, Alvin. "Children Need Attention and Reassurance, Harvard Researchers Say." *Harvard Gazette*, 9 Apr. 1998. (link available)

20 Middlemiss, Wendy, et al. "Asynchrony of Mother–Infant Hypothalamic–Pituitary–Adrenal Axis Activity Following Extinction of Infant Crying Responses Induced during the Transition to Sleep." *Early Human Development*, vol. 88, no. 4, 2012, pp. 227–232., doi:10.1016/j.earlhumdev.2011.08.010. (link available)

21 Price, A. M. H., et al. "Five-Year Follow-up of Harms and Benefits of Behavioral Infant Sleep Intervention: Randomized Trial." *Pediatrics*, vol. 130, no. 4, Oct. 2012, pp. 643–651., doi:10.1542/peds.2011-3467. (link available)

22 Jha, Alok. "Why Crying Babies Are So Hard to Ignore." *The Guardian*, Guardian News and Media, 17 Oct. 2012. (link available)

[23]   Johnson, Jeremy D., et al. "Infantile Colic: Recognition and Treatment." *American Family Physician*, 1 Oct. 2015. (link available)

[24]   Johnson, Jeremy D., et al. "Infantile Colic: Recognition and Treatment." *American Family Physician*, 1 Oct. 2015. (link available)

[25]   Barr, Marilyn. "What Is the Period of PURPLE Crying?" *The Period of PURPLE Crying.* (link available)

[26]   "Colic Relief Tips for Parents." *HealthyChildren.org*, American Academy of Pediatrics, 24 June 2015. (link available)

[27]   Jakobsson, Iréne, and Tor Lindberg. "Cow's Milk Proteins Cause Infantile Colic in Breast-Fed Infants: A Double-Blind Crossover Study." *Pediatrics*, vol. 71, no. 2, Feb. 1983 pp. 268-271. (link available)

[28]   Adler, Liora. "Colic and Crying - Self-Care: MedlinePlus Medical Encyclopedia." *MedlinePlus*, U.S. National Library of Medicine, 7 Mar. 2019. (link available)

[29]   "Colic Relief Tips for Parents." *HealthyChildren.org*, American Academy of Pediatrics, 24 June 2015. (link available)

[30]   Botha, Elina, et al. "The Consequences of Having an Excessively Crying Infant in the Family: an Integrative Literature Review." *Wiley Online Library*, John Wiley & Sons, Ltd, 6 May 2019, doi:10.1111/scs.12702. (link available)

31 "Shaken Baby Syndrome." *AANS*, American Association of Neurological Surgeons. (link available)

32 "Dunstan Baby Language." *Wikipedia*, Wikimedia Foundation, 30 Mar. 2020. (link available)

33 "Our Research." *Baby Language by DBL*. (link available)

34 Novak, Sara. "What's the Right Temperature for Baby?" *What to Expect*, 1 Apr. 2020. (link available)

35 "SIDS and Other Sleep-Related Infant Deaths: Updated 2016 Recommendations for a Safe Infant Sleeping Environment." *Pediatrics*, vol. 138, no. 5, Nov. 2016, doi:10.1542/peds.2016-2938. (link available)

36 "Fever." *Raising Children Network*, 14 Aug. 2019. (link available)

37 Leduc, D, and S Woods. "Temperature Measurement in Paediatrics." *Paediatrics & Child Health*, vol. 5, no. 5, 2000, pp. 273–276., doi:10.1093/pch/5.5.273. (link available)

38 "Babies: How Can You Tell If Your Baby Is Ill?" *About Kids Health*, 7 Jan. 2019. (link available)

39 Bruel, Ann Van Den, et al. "Diagnostic Value of Clinical Features at Presentation to Identify Serious Infection in Children in Developed Countries: a Systematic Review." *The Lancet*, vol. 375, no. 9717, 6 Mar. 2010, pp. 834–845., doi:10.1016/s0140-6736(09)62000-6. (link available)

40   Northrup, Christiane. *Mother-Daughter Wisdom: Creating a Legacy of Physical and Emotional Health*. Piatkus, 2005, p. 119 – 121

41   "WHO Recommendation on Skin-to-Skin Contact during the First Hour after Birth." *World Health Organization*, WHO, 17 Feb. 2018. (link available)

42   Shorey, Shefaly, et al. "Skin-to-Skin Contact by Fathers and the Impact on Infant and Paternal Outcomes: an Integrative Review." *Midwifery*, vol. 40, Sept. 2016, pp. 207–217., doi:10.1016/j.midw.2016.07.007. (link available)

43   Robinson, A. "Skin to Skin Contact." *NHS Royal Berkshire*, Royal Berkshire NHS Foundation Trust, 29 May 2019. (link available)

44   Bergland, Christopher. "More Proof That Skin-to-Skin Contact Benefits Babies Brains." *Psychology Today*, Sussex Publishers, 16 Mar. 2017. (link available)

45   Crenshaw, Jeannette T. "Healthy Birth Practice #6: Keep Mother and Baby Together— It's Best for Mother, Baby, and Breastfeeding." *The Journal of Perinatal Education*, vol. 23, no. 4, 2014, pp. 211–217., doi:10.1891/1058-1243.23.4.211. (link available)

46   "Recovering from Delivery - Postpartum Recovery." *Familydoctor.org*, 26 Sept. 2018. (link available)

47   "Exercise After Pregnancy." *ACOG*, American College of Obstetricians and Gynecologists. (link available)

48 "Hair Loss in New Moms." *American Academy of Dermatology.* (link available)

49 "Perinatal Depression." *National Institute of Mental Health*, U.S. Department of Health and Human Services. (link available)

50 Paulson, James F., and Sharnail D. Bazemore. "Prenatal and Postpartum Depression in Fathers and Its Association with Maternal Depression." *Jama*, vol. 303, no. 19, 19 May 2010, pp. 1961–1969., doi:10.1001/jama.2010.605. (link available)

51 Jaworski, Margaret. "Oh Baby: Postpartum Depression in Men Is Real, Science Says." *Psycom*, 14 May 2019. (link available)

52 "Mastitis." *Australian Breastfeeding Association*, Sept. 2019. (link available)

53 "Mastitis." *Mayo Clinic*, Mayo Foundation for Medical Education and Research, 19 July 2018. (link available)

54 "Mastitis." *Australian Breastfeeding Association*, Sept. 2019. (link available)

55 "Blocked Ducts." *Australian Breastfeeding Association*, June 2016. (link available)

56 "Mastitis." *La Leche League International.* (link available)

57 Lavigne, Valérie, and Brian J. Gleberzon. "Ultrasound as a Treatment of Mammary Blocked Duct among 25 Postpartum Lactating Women: a Retrospective Case Series." *Journal of Chiropractic Medicine*, vol. 11, no. 3,

Sept. 2012, pp. 170–178., doi:10.1016/j.jcm.2012.05.011. (link available)

[58] "Mastitis." *La Leche League International*. (link available)

[59] "White Spot on the Nipple." *Australian Breastfeeding Association*, Mar. 2015. (link available)

[60] "White Spot on the Nipple." *Australian Breastfeeding Association*, Mar. 2015. (link available)

[61] "Mastitis." *La Leche League International*. (link available)

[62] Bonyata, Kelly. "Lecithin Treatment for Recurrent Plugged Ducts" *KellyMom*, 1 Jan. 2018. (link available)

[63] "Mastitis." *Australian Breastfeeding Association*, Sept. 2019. (link available)

[64] Diez-Sampedro, Ana, et al. "Women's Choice Regarding Breastfeeding and Its Effect on Well-Being." *Nursing for Womens Health*, vol. 23, no. 5, Oct. 2019, pp. 383–389., doi:10.1016/j.nwh.2019.08.002. (link available)

[65] "Breastfeeding Report Card." *CDC*, Centers for Disease Control and Prevention, 31 Dec. 2019. (link available)

[66] Cacho, Nicole Theresa, and Robert M. Lawrence. "Innate Immunity and Breast Milk." *Frontiers in Immunology*, vol. 8, 29 May 2017, doi:10.3389/fimmu.2017.00584. (link available)

[67] Slade, Herbert, and Stanley Schwartz. "Mucosal Immunity: the Immunology of Breast Milk." *Journal of Allergy and Clinical Immunology*, vol. 80, no. 3, Sept. 1987,

pp. 348–358., doi:10.1016/0091-6749(87)90041-8. (link available)

[68] Bjarnadottir, Adda. "11 Benefits of Breastfeeding for Both Mom and Baby." *Healthline Parenthood*, Red Ventures, 1 June 2017. (link available)

[69] Belfort, Mandy Brown. "The Science of Breastfeeding and Brain Development." *Breastfeeding Medicine*, vol. 12, no. 8, 1 Oct. 2017, pp. 459–461., doi:10.1089/bfm.2017.0122. (link available)

[70] Kramer, Michael S. "Breastfeeding and Child Cognitive Development." *Archives of General Psychiatry*, vol. 65, no. 5, 1 May 2008, p. 578., doi:10.1001/archpsyc.65.5.578. (link available)

[71] Der, Geoff, et al. "Effect of Breast Feeding on Intelligence in Children: Prospective Study, Sibling Pairs Analysis, and Meta-Analysis." *Bmj*, vol. 333, no. 7575, 4 Oct. 2006, p. 945., doi:10.1136/bmj.38978.699583.55. (link available)

[72] Thompson, John M.d., et al. "Duration of Breastfeeding and Risk of SIDS: An Individual Participant Data Meta-Analysis." *Pediatrics*, vol. 140, no. 5, 30 Oct. 2017, doi:10.1542/peds.2017-1324. (link available)

[73] Anstey, Erica H., et al. "Breastfeeding and Breast Cancer Risk Reduction: Implications for Black Mothers." *American Journal of Preventive Medicine*, vol. 53, no. 3, Sept. 2017, doi:10.1016/j.amepre.2017.04.024. (link available)

74 "Breast Cancer and Breastfeeding: Collaborative Reanalysis of Individual Data from 47 Epidemiological Studies in 30 Countries, Including 50 302 Women with Breast Cancer and 96 973 Women without the Disease." *The Lancet*, vol. 360, no. 9328, July 2002, pp. 187–195., doi:10.1016/s0140-6736(02)09454-0. (link available)

75 Jarlenski, Marian P., et al. "Effects of Breastfeeding on Postpartum Weight Loss among U.S. Women." *Preventive Medicine*, vol. 69, 5 Oct. 2014, pp. 146–150., doi:10.1016/j.ypmed.2014.09.018. (link available)

76 "Breastfeeding: Surgeon General's Call to Action Fact Sheet." *HHS.gov*, US Department of Health and Human Services, 19 Jan. 2011. (link available)

77 Hotham, Neil, and Elizabeth Hotham. "Drugs in Breastfeeding." *Australian Prescriber*, vol. 38, no. 5, 1 Oct. 2015, pp. 156–159., doi:10.18773/austprescr.2015.056. (link available)

78 "Alcohol." *CDC*, Centers for Disease Control and Prevention, 28 Dec. 2019. (link available)

79 Spencer, Jeanne. "Management of Mastitis in Breastfeeding Women." *American Family Physician*, vol. 78, no. 6, 15 Sept. 2008, pp. 727–731. (link available)

[80] Chao, S. "The Effect of Lactation on Ovulation and
      Fertility." *Clinics in Perinatology*, vol. 14, no. 1, Mar. 1987,
      pp. 39–50. (link available)

[81] Anokye, Reindolf, et al. "Prevalence of Postpartum
      Depression and Interventions Utilized for Its
      Management." *Annals of General Psychiatry*, vol. 17, no. 1,
      9 May 2018, doi:10.1186/s12991-018-0188-0. (link
      available)

[82] Kramer, Michael S, and Ritsuko Kakuma. "Optimal
      Duration of Exclusive Breastfeeding." *Cochrane Database of
      Systematic Reviews*, 15 Aug. 2012,
      doi:10.1002/14651858.cd003517.pub2. (link available)

[83] Mcleod, Saul. "Jean Piaget's Theory of Cognitive
      Development." *Simply Psychology*, 6 June 2018. (link
      available)

[84] Weerth, C., and P. Geert. "Emotional Instability as an
      Indicator of Strictly Timed Infantile Developmental
      Transitions." *British Journal of Developmental Psychology*,
      vol. 16, no. 1, Mar. 1998, pp. 15–44., doi:10.1111/j.2044-
      835x.1998.tb00748.x. (link available)

[85] Jando, G., et al. "Early-Onset Binocularity in Preterm
      Infants Reveals Experience-Dependent Visual
      Development in Humans." *Proceedings of the National
      Academy of Sciences*, vol. 109, no. 27, 18 June 2012, pp.
      11049–11052., doi:10.1073/pnas.1203096109. (link
      available)

86 "Age-Appropriate Vision Milestones." *Stanford Children's Health*, Lucile Packard Children's Hospital Stanford. (link available)

87 "Age-Appropriate Vision Milestones." *Stanford Children's Health*, Lucile Packard Children's Hospital Stanford. (link available)

88 "Age-Appropriate Vision Milestones." *Stanford Children's Health*, Lucile Packard Children's Hospital Stanford. (link available)

89 Bushneil, I. W. R., et al. "Neonatal Recognition of the Mothers Face." *British Journal of Developmental Psychology*, vol. 7, no. 1, Mar. 1989, pp. 3–15., doi:10.1111/j.2044-835x.1989.tb00784.x. (link available)

90 Hyvärinen, Lea, et al. "Current Understanding of What Infants See." *Current Ophthalmology Reports*, vol. 2, no. 4, 25 Oct. 2014, pp. 142–149., doi:10.1007/s40135-014-0056-2. (link available)

91 Heiting, Gary. "How to Spot Vision Problems in Babies." *All About Vision*, Apr. 2017. (link available)

92 "0-1 Month: Newborn Development." *Raising Children Network*, 13 Mar. 2020. (link available)

93 "Age-Appropriate Vision Milestones." *Stanford Children's Health*, Lucile Packard Children's Hospital Stanford. (link available)

94 "Age-Appropriate Vision Milestones." *Stanford Children's Health*, Lucile Packard Children's Hospital Stanford. (link available)

95 "Language Development: 3-12 Months." *Raising Children Network*, 27 Nov. 2017. (link available)

96 Brink, Susan. *The Fourth Trimester: Understanding, Protecting and Nurturing an Infant through the First Three Months*. University of California Press, 2013.

97 "Talking with Babies and Toddlers: How to Do It and Why." *Raising Children Network*, 19 Nov. 2019. (link available)

98 "Language Development: Speech Milestones for Babies." *Mayo Clinic*, Mayo Foundation for Medical Education and Research, 7 Mar. 2019. (link available)

99 Thompson, Rachel H., et al. "Enhancing Early Communication Through Infant Sign Training." *Journal of Applied Behavior Analysis*, vol. 40, no. 1, Mar. 2007, pp. 15–23., doi:10.1901/jaba.2007.23-06. (link available)

100 Loos, Helene M., et al. "Responses of Human Neonates to Highly Diluted Odorants from Sweat." *Journal of Chemical Ecology*, vol. 43, no. 1, Jan. 2017, pp. 106–117., doi:10.1007/s10886-016-0804-x. (link available)

101 Vaglio, Stefano. "Chemical Communication and Mother-Infant Recognition." *Communicative & Integrative Biology*, vol. 2, no. 3, May 2009, pp. 279–281., doi:10.4161/cib.2.3.8227. (link available)

[102] "Let's Play! 4 Weeks." *BabyCenter Australia*. (link available)

[103] Mersch, John. "Infant Milestones Chart Month by Month - Is Your Baby Hitting the Marks?" *EMedicineHealth*, 30 Sept. 2019. (link available)

[104] "Newborn Reflexes." *HealthyChildren.org*, American Academy of Pediatrics, 1 Aug. 2009. (link available)

[105] Mersch, John. "Infant Milestones Chart Month by Month - Is Your Baby Hitting the Marks?" *EMedicineHealth*, 30 Sept. 2019. (link available)

[106] "Back to Sleep, Tummy to Play." *HealthyChildren.org*, American Academy of Pediatrics, 20 Jan. 2017. (link available)

[107] Ritchie, Hannah, and Samantha Vanderslott. "How Many People Support Vaccination across the World?" Our World in Data, 1 Aug. 2019. (link available)

[108] "History of Anti-Vaccination Movements." *History of Vaccines*, 10 Jan. 2018. (link available)

[109] "Vaccine Basics." *CDC*, Centers for Disease Control and Prevention, 12 July 2017. (link available)

[110] Mckee, Chephra, and Kristin Bohannon. "Exploring the Reasons Behind Parental Refusal of Vaccines." *The Journal of Pediatric Pharmacology and Therapeutics*, vol. 21, no. 2, Apr. 2016, pp. 104–109., doi:10.5863/1551-6776-21.2.104. (link available)

111 "About The AVN." *Australian Vaccination-Risks Network Inc.* (link available)

112 Wakefield, Aj, et al. "RETRACTED: Ileal-Lymphoid-Nodular Hyperplasia, Non-Specific Colitis, and Pervasive Developmental Disorder in Children." *The Lancet*, vol. 351, no. 9103, Feb. 1998, pp. 637–641., doi:10.1016/s0140-6736(97)11096-0. (link available)

113 Godlee, F., et al. "Wakefields Article Linking MMR Vaccine and Autism Was Fraudulent." *Bmj*, vol. 342, no. jan05 1, 5 Jan. 2011, pp. c7452–c7452., doi:10.1136/bmj.c7452. (link available)

114 Dyer, Owen. "Wakefield Admits Fabricating Events When He Took Children's Blood Samples." *Bmj*, vol. 336, no. 7649, 17 Apr. 2008, doi:10.1136/bmj.39553.506597.db. (link available)

115 Murch, Simon H, et al. "Retraction of an Interpretation." *The Lancet*, vol. 363, no. 9411, Mar. 2004, p. 750., doi:10.1016/s0140-6736(04)15715-2. (link available)

116 Meikle, James, and Sarah Boseley. "MMR Row Doctor Andrew Wakefield Struck off Register." *The Guardian*, Guardian News and Media, 24 May 2010. (link available)

117 Boseley, Sarah. "How Disgraced Anti-Vaxxer Andrew Wakefield Was Embraced by Trump's America." *The Guardian*, Guardian News and Media, 18 July 2018. (link available)

118 "Thimerosal." *DrugBank*, 1 Mar. 2020. (link available)

119 "Thimerosal in Vaccines." *CDC*, Centers for Disease
     Control and Prevention, 27 Oct. 2015. (link available)

120 "Are Vaccines Safe?" *Health.gov.au*, Australian
     Government Department of Health, 18 Nov. 2019. (link
     available)

121 "Vaccine Ingredients." *Vaccine Knowledge Project*,
     University of Oxford, Aug. 2019. (link available)

122 "What Goes Into a Vaccine?" *PublicHealth.org*,
     PublicHealth.org, 14 Apr. 2020. (link available)

123 "What's in Vaccines?" *CDC*, Centers for Disease Control
     and Prevention, 5 Aug. 2019. (link available)

124 "Thimerosal." *DrugBank*, 1 Mar. 2020. (link available)

125 "Adjuvants Help Vaccines Work Better." *CDC*, Centers
     for Disease Control and Prevention, 24 Oct. 2018. (link
     available)

126 "What's in Vaccines?" *CDC*, Centers for Disease Control
     and Prevention, 5 Aug. 2019. (link available)

127 "What Goes Into a Vaccine?" *PublicHealth.org*,
     PublicHealth.org, 14 Apr. 2020. (link available)

128 "Public Health Statement for Aluminum." *Agency for Toxic
     Substances & Disease Registry*, Centers for Disease Control
     and Prevention, Sept. 2008. (link available)

129 "What Goes Into a Vaccine?" *PublicHealth.org*,
     PublicHealth.org, 14 Apr. 2020. (link available)

[130] "What Goes Into a Vaccine?" *PublicHealth.org*, PublicHealth.org, 14 Apr. 2020. (link available)

[131] Farrell, D J. "Fatal Water Intoxication." *Journal of Clinical Pathology*, vol. 56, no. 10, 1 Oct. 2003, doi:10.1136/jcp.56.10.803-a. (link available)

[132] Chawla, Anuj, and Ak Lavania. "Oxygen Toxicity." *Medical Journal Armed Forces India*, vol. 57, no. 2, Apr. 2001, pp. 131–133., doi:10.1016/s0377-1237(01)80133-7. (link available)

[133] Principi, Nicola, and Susanna Esposito. "Aluminum in Vaccines: Does It Create a Safety Problem?" *Vaccine*, vol. 36, no. 39, Sept. 2018, pp. 5825–5831., doi:10.1016/j.vaccine.2018.08.036. (link available)

[134] Principi, Nicola, and Susanna Esposito. "Aluminum in Vaccines: Does It Create a Safety Problem?" *Vaccine*, vol. 36, no. 39, Sept. 2018, pp. 5825–5831., 10.1016/j.vaccine.2018.08.036. (link available)

[135] "Six Common Misconceptions about Immunization." *World Health Organization*, World Health Organization, Sept. 2019. (link available)

[136] Funk, Sebastian. "Critical immunity thresholds for measles elimination" *World Health Organization*, PDF. 19 Oct. 2017. (link available)

[137] "Childhood Immunisation Coverage." *Health.gov.au*, Australian Government Department of Health, 15 Feb. 2020. (link available)

138 "Statue Commemorates Smallpox Eradication." *World Health Organization*, WHO, 10 Dec. 2010. (link available)

139 "Diseases You Almost Forgot About (Thanks to Vaccines)." *CDC*, Centers for Disease Control and Prevention, 3 Jan. 2020. (link available)

140 "Preventing and Managing Adverse Reactions." *CDC*, Centers for Disease Control and Prevention, 12 July 2017. (link available)

141 "How Dangerous Is Lightning?" *National Weather Service*, NOAA's National Weather Service, 12 Mar. 2019. (link available)

142 "Vaccine Myths Debunked." *PublicHealth.org*, 14 Apr. 2020. (link available)

143 Taylor, Brent, et al. "Autism and Measles, Mumps, and Rubella Vaccine: No Epidemiological Evidence for a Causal Association." *The Lancet*, vol. 353, no. 9169, 12 June 1999, pp. 2026–2029., doi:10.1016/s0140-6736(99)01239-8. (link available)

144 Dales, Loring. "Time Trends in Autism and in MMR Immunization Coverage in California." *Jama*, vol. 285, no. 9, 7 Mar. 2001, pp. 1183–1185., doi:10.1001/jama.285.9.1183. (link available)

145 Madsen, Kreesten Meldgaard, et al. "A Population-Based Study of Measles, Mumps, and Rubella Vaccination and Autism." *New England Journal of Medicine*, vol. 347, no.

19, 7 Nov. 2002, pp. 1477–1482.,
doi:10.1056/nejmoa021134. (link available)

[146] Fombonne, E., et al. "Pervasive Developmental Disorders in Montreal, Quebec, Canada: Prevalence and Links With Immunizations." *Pediatrics*, vol. 118, no. 1, 1 July 2006, pp. e139–e150., doi:10.1542/peds.2005-2993. (link available)

[147] Heron, J. "Thimerosal Exposure in Infants and Developmental Disorders: A Prospective Cohort Study in the United Kingdom Does Not Support a Causal Association." *Pediatrics*, vol. 114, no. 3, Sept. 2004, pp. 577–583., doi:10.1542/peds.2003-1176-1. (link available)

[148] "Vaccine Safety: Examine the Evidence." *HealthyChildren.org*, American Academy of Pediatrics, 24 July 2018. (link available)

[149] Willinger, Marian, et al. "Defining the Sudden Infant Death Syndrome (Sids): Deliberations of an Expert Panel Convened by the National Institute of Child Health and Human Development." *Pediatric Pathology*, vol. 11, no. 5, Jan. 1991, pp. 677–684., doi:10.3109/15513819109065465. (link available)

[150] Heron, Melonie. "Deaths: Leading Causes for 2013." *National Vital Statistics Reports*, PDF, 16 Feb. 2016. (link available)

[151] "SIDS and Other Sleep-Related Infant Deaths: Updated 2016 Recommendations for a Safe Infant Sleeping

Environment." *Pediatrics*, vol. 138, no. 5, 24 Oct. 2016, doi:10.1542/peds.2016-2938. (link available)

[152] Moon, Rachel Y. "SIDS and Other Sleep-Related Infant Deaths: Evidence Base for 2016 Updated Recommendations for a Safe Infant Sleeping Environment." *Pediatrics*, vol. 138, no. 5, 24 Oct. 2016, doi:10.1542/peds.2016-2940. (link available)

[153] Hauck, F. R., et al. "Breastfeeding and Reduced Risk of Sudden Infant Death Syndrome: A Meta-Analysis." *Pediatrics*, vol. 128, no. 1, 13 June 2011, pp. 103–110., doi:10.1542/peds.2010-3000. (link available)

[154] Oster, Emily. *Cribsheet: a Data-Driven Guide to Better, More Relaxed Parenting, from Birth to Preschool.* Souvenir Press, 2020. Chapter 6. (link available)

[155] "Substance Use During Pregnancy." *CDC*, Centers for Disease Control and Prevention, 24 July 2019. (link available)

[156] Mitchell, E.a., and J. Milerad. "Smoking and the Sudden Infant Death Syndrome." *Reviews on Environmental Health*, vol. 21, no. 2, Jan. 2006, pp. 81–103., doi:10.1515/reveh.2006.21.2.81. (link available)

[157] "SIDS and Other Sleep-Related Infant Deaths: Updated 2016 Recommendations for a Safe Infant Sleeping Environment." *Pediatrics*, vol. 138, no. 5, 24 Oct. 2016, doi:10.1542/peds.2016-2938. (link available)

158 "Room Temperature." *Red Nose Australia*, 27 Feb. 2018. (link available)

159 Mitchell, E A, et al. "Immunisation and the Sudden Infant Death Syndrome. New Zealand Cot Death Study Group." *Archives of Disease in Childhood*, vol. 73, no. 6, 1 Dec. 1995, pp. 498–501., doi:10.1136/adc.73.6.498. (link available)

160 "SIDS and Other Sleep-Related Infant Deaths: Updated 2016 Recommendations for a Safe Infant Sleeping Environment." *Pediatrics*, vol. 138, no. 5, 24 Oct. 2016, doi:10.1542/peds.2016-2938. (link available)

161 Jay L. Hoecker, M.D. "How Can I Protect My Baby from Infant Botulism?" *Mayo Clinic*, Mayo Foundation for Medical Education and Research, 15 May 2018. (link available)

162 "Family Planning/Contraception." *World Health Organization*, WHO, 8 Feb. 2018. (link available)

163 Mcdonald, Ea, and Sj Brown. "Does Method of Birth Make a Difference to When Women Resume Sex after Childbirth?" *BJOG: An International Journal of Obstetrics & Gynaecology*, vol. 120, no. 7, 27 Feb. 2013, pp. 823–830., doi:10.1111/1471-0528.12166. (link available)

164 Gilmour, Kim. "How to Buy the Best Pram or Stroller for Your Baby." *CHOICE*, 19 Sept. 2019. (link available)

[165] Blaiklock, Ken. "Talking with Children When Using Prams While Shopping." *NZ Research in Early Childhood Education Journal*, vol. 16, 2013, pp. 15–28. (link available)

[166] Zeedyk, Suzanne. "How Buggies Shape Babies' Brains." *Suzanne Zeedyk*, 3 Apr. 2014. (link available)

[167] Zeedyk, Suzanne. "How Buggies Shape Babies' Brains." *Suzanne Zeedyk*, 3 Apr. 2014. (link available)

[168] Genna, Catherine Watson, and Diklah Barak. "Facilitating Autonomous Infant Hand Use During Breastfeeding." *Clinical Lactation*, vol. 1, no. 1, Oct. 2010, pp. 15–20., doi:10.1891/215805310807011846. (link available)

[169] Korioth, Trisha. "Safe and Sound: Tips for Using Infant Swings." *AAP News*, vol. 34, no. 1, 1 Jan. 2013. (link available)

[170] "Exercise for Stress and Anxiety." *Anxiety and Depression Association of America, ADAA.* (link available)

[171] Warburton, D. E. R. "Health Benefits of Physical Activity: The Evidence." *Canadian Medical Association Journal*, vol. 174, no. 6, 14 Mar. 2006, pp. 801–809., doi:10.1503/cmaj.051351. (link available)

Made in the USA
Coppell, TX
14 May 2021

55642684R00174